My Life Story

My Life Story

K.G. Gupta

authorHOUSE®

AuthorHouse™
1663 Liberty Drive
Bloomington, IN 47403
www.authorhouse.com
Phone: 1-800-839-8640

Published by AuthorHouse   12/18/2012

ISBN: 978-1-4772-9917-3 (sc)
ISBN: 978-1-4772-9915-9 (hc)
ISBN: 978-1-4772-9916-6 (e)

Library of Congress Control Number: 2012923549

Contents

Preface xi

Part One

My life story from 1939 to 1964 3
My eldest sister Shakuntala...9
Daulatganj middle school 10
My teachers 12
Games and adventures 13
Temple Of Palebaba 16
Arbi Ke Patte 18
Gulmohar tree..19
In between 1953 and 1955 three events took place...............20
Maharajwarah High School 21
My second elder sister Maya...24
End of golden period of my life 26
Sinhasan of Vikramaditya..27
Harsiddhi Devi Temple...28
River Shipra 31
Dutt ka Akhara 33
Sandipani Ashram 35
Garh ki Kalika 36
Temple of Bhairavbaba..38
Cave of Raja Bhartari 39
Madhav College Ujjain...41
Satin Desai, O.P. Kaushik and the final match of football
    that I will never forget...42
National Cadet Corps 44

My friend Mangilal Gupta...46

My college union activities..47

My act of theft..48

My suspension from college 49

Employees State Insurance Corporation (ESIC)..................51

Mr. Bhargava a kind gentleman..52

Regional Director Mr. A.N. Bidani 53

Mr. R.R.Mishra Manager Local Office of E.S.I.

    Corporation Ujjain..55

Back to my old College..56

Life in Namli..58

Sailana..60

A boy who often comes in my dream.................................62

Opium fields..64

My transfer to district school and Suneel William 65

Termination of my services 67

My Friend Shri Narendra Jain...68

My friend Babu Maheshwari 69

Part Two

My life story from 1965 to 1980 73

Arrival in Bombay 73

First lesson I learnt 75

Mr. Motisingh Chauhan..77

Bachelor life in Bombay...79

Our Picnic to Trimbakeshwar a Jyotirlinga temple..............81

My reading in Bombay..82

My promotion and marriage with Sumitra...........................83

Sumitra's arrival in Mumbai 85

Birth of my first son Sundeep 87

My health problem 88

God again helped me 89

Influence of Shri Harishankar Dwivedi Tauji on my life...........91

Promotion as Accountant..93

Munni daughter of Shri Rudradutta Gupta (dada) 94

Shri V.N. Khanna 95

Transfer to Calcutta 96

How I gained knowledge of labour Laws 97

A threatening letter 99

Sundeep fractured his leg..100

Back to Bombay 101

Rajendra Somani..102

Transferred to Nasik 103

Shri. Susheel Somani...104

God called me for Darshan.......................................105

Again I had Darshan..107

My job and colleagues...108

Mrs and Mr Sunder, their son Niketh and their
      daughter Neena 111

Mr. Shriram Damle and his daughter Sarita 113

Laksh Chandi Yagna was performed...............................115

Visit of The Dada (Pandurangji Shashtri Ahavale)...............116

Great event and a test of my organizational skill.................117

Bismillakhan Saheb 119

Talat Mahmood 120

Fire by short circuit and Dance of Gopikrishna....................121

Yusuf Azad and Mahelka Banau..................................123

Construction of two buildings for members of staff................125

Paper project 127

Shri Clay Products...129

Part Three

My life story from 1981 to 1990 133

Shri Clay products 133

Again I was called by K.K. Babu and my appointment

    as General Manager..134

My first day at factory site...136

Shri N. L. Bhatia 138

H. S. Makwana 139

My dilemma 141

My stay at the site..143

Shri B.M. Agrawal of Agrawal oil Mills Bhusawal............145

Shri Madhukarrao Chaudhari 148

Construction of labour quarters 150

Inauguration..152

Shri S.B.Bhutada 153

Shri P.K.Chopra 154

Erection of pulp mills 155

Sanjay Dharde...157

Shri Arun Somani...159

Shri Hanumansingh Gahlot 160

Leva Patils Community..161

Shri V. Sheshadrirao...162

Shri P.K. Chopra and his three Musketeers........................166

Dayaram Devram Sonawane 168

Children of colony...172

Chemical recovery boiler and my Europe tour 173

Sundeep again 176

Development of colony 177

Transfer of children to Nasik for education 178

Shri. Vinodchandra C. Parekh 181

Labour unrest and lockout 185

Inauguration of a "Pyauu" 194

Shri N.L. Mishra, Commercial Manager 195

Smooth working thereafter 196

Partition and my departure from Bhusawal 198

Part Four

My life story from 1991 to 2012 203

Registration of Trust 206

Marriage of Sundeep 207

My first visit to USA 208

Real break in business 213

Purchase of plots of land and construction of bungalow 215

Sudden shock from Amit 217

First Building of Golden Horizon School 220

Second Building of Golden Horizon School 224

Mrs. Shaila Thomas 228

Permission for Higher Secondary School 230

Dedication of teachers 232

Marriage of Amit 234

Good neighbor Mr. T.P.Bhagwat 235

Manohar Gardens Residents Welfare Association 237

Temple of Laxminarayan 240

Shri Kanhaiya Kalani known as Kanu Kalani 241

Our family friend Mr Vijay Bhutani and
    Mrs Veena Bhutani and why we like them 242

Our project named as Last Bed (Antim Shhayya) 2009 244

Shri G.K.Chaddha a social worker 247

My old friend Devichand and his daughter Ritu 249

Senior Madhvians' Meet 250

Sharad Bapat my old college friend......................251

My two neighbours worth a mention here...........254

My wife Sumitra Gupta 255

Chairman's day...257

The best gift I ever received 258

The Grand Lodge of India.................................260

Life now 262

PREFACE

When at first the idea of writing my life story came to my mind, I asked myself what is there in my life story and why should I write it? I have neither become a celebrity nor achieved something remarkable that is useful to society. This self-raised question delayed the idea of writing this book for almost 5 years. However, I was unable to resist the temptation of writing. One day when I was speaking over the phone with my elder sister, Maya Jain who lives in New Delhi, I shared with her this thought that was troubling my mind for long. She admired it and encouraged me, but still I felt that my question remained unanswered.

Later my daughters-in-law also liked the idea. One of them Vallary, from Bombay, provided me the answer. She told me that if I write this autobiography my children will at least know about their family members and great grand children about their roots. I decided in favour of writing my story.

Then there came the difficult task of collecting data. My eldest sister Shankuntla, who lives in Jaipur provided me with answers to many questions. She wrote her memories covering my grandfather, nanaji and my life in 19 hand written pages. Without her help I would not have completed this work.

My sister Maya filled in the remaining blanks.

This is a life story of a person who passed through many difficulties but ultimately could achieve a position that he never imagined. It is a story of a common man that tells that how fate plays its part in one's life. What he thinks he may achieve but God gives him always something better. How God comes to his rescue whenever he is in trouble. This is a story that cultivates enormous faith in God. Ultimately it is a message that you can achieve only what God has written in your destiny but there is no substitute for hard work. You must perform first and then taste the fruits of your hard work.

Nasik Road

July 12, 2012

(K. G. Gupta)

PART ONE

MY LIFE STORY
FROM 1939 TO 1964

When I became capable of recognizing things around me I found myself in the city of Ujjain. Much later in life I was told that I was born in Murar a city near Gwalior. But my love for Ujjain was so deep that whenever I was asked where I was born and brought up, I invariably said "Ujjain!" My father was in the Land Record office of Scindia State and he was transferred from Gwalior to Ujjain in 1941 as the Officer-in-charge. He had studied Urdu language. During that time all land records were written in Urdu. My father told us the story of how he got the employment. After passing Urdu middle examination he came to see the city of Gwalior. Alighting from the train, he read a notice at the station. It said that any person with the knowledge of Urdu language is required in the Land Record office of Scindia State. My father went to the office and was immediately appointed. After some time he was transferred to Ujjain as the Officer-in-charge of Land Record Office. At that time we were four siblings. I had two elder sisters and one elder brother.

In Ujjain we stayed in a big bungalow. The bungalow belonged to the owner of a Cotton Ginning factory. The factory was situated in approximately 50 acres of land. The factory was not in operation. I do not know when it was shutdown. It must have been some time before 1940. We stayed in this bungalow from 1941 to 1955.

My Fufaji was the Chief Engineer of this factory. He was from a very rich family and studied engineering at Aligarh Muslim University. He was the most trusted employee of Seth Shri Laxmandas Ji, the owner of the factory. He had established this factory and also erected four to five other factories. Unfortunately he died at the age of 39. Since Sethji was very busy with other factories and he could not find any other reliable person the factory was closed down on account of mis-management. The bungalow was lying vacant and no one take care of the assets of the closed factory. Sethji advised my father to stay in that bungalow and take care of the factory while continuing his job. My father agreed. It was the golden period of my life. I considered that life was beautiful. We stayed there from 1941 to 1955 till the factory was sold. The land was on leasehold and was subsequently occupied by the Civil Hospital of Ujjain.

The house in which we were staying was really a palatial one. It must have been ten to fifteen thousand square feet of built up area. On the walls of the main hall many beautiful paintings were still to be found. We kept several rooms closed. I still remember the layout. Sometimes I think that the house made such an everlasting impression on me that when I constructed my own house in Nasik it was similar to that bungalow.

Layout of bungalow in which my childhood was spent.

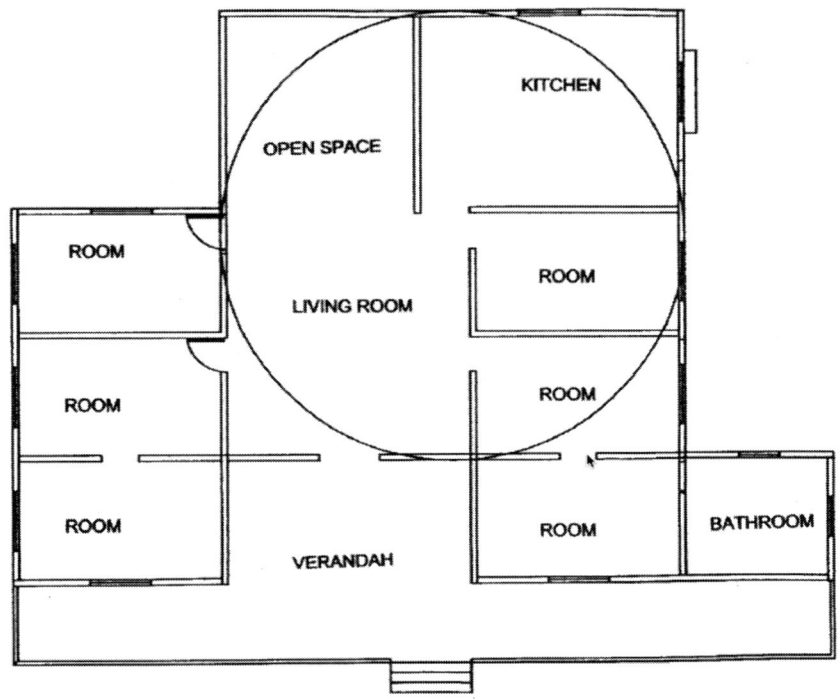

I once asked my father why the kitchen was so big. He explained that when the factory was in operation the kitchen was used to serve many people employed at the factory.

Earlier I mentioned that this was the golden period of my life. The reason was that I grew up amidst nature and in a place that had a large area for playing. I had the entire 50 acres at my disposal for playing games. I was enjoying Mother Nature at it's best.

About 100 meters away from our bungalow to the Northwest, there were a few living quarters, perhaps as many as 10 to 15, where some of the labourers from the factory that had shutdown were living. They also had school-age children. They all became my playmates. I still remember a few names—Baban, Kamlakar, Laxman, Rajaram and Pannalal.

Since the factory had shutdown for a long time, wild growth had taken place. In the rainy season it was full of different kind of flowers everywhere, and it gave the appearance of a "valley of flowers". Flocks of butterflies of different colours arrived. No one knew where they came from and where they'd go. The beautiful and colourful flowers and butterflies that I had seen in those days, were never seen by me later, though I have visited several reserve forests.

At that time, life was beautiful without any worry. There was no playgroup, nursery, junior K.G or senior. K.G.

There was nothing to do except play. The whole day was at my disposal. In those days each couple had many children so they could not keep close watch on them all. I would play with my friends. Sometime catching butterflies, sometimes hide and seek and many other games like swirling the top, hitting the marbles with a taw (big marble) and collecting as many as possible, tip-cat (gulli danda), hop-scotch (stapu), seven tiles (pithu) and chor-police (hide & seek).

There was a fountain by the side of our bungalow. It was about four feet deep but the water connection had been removed. It was dry. It must have been in operation when the factory was working. We used to jump inside it. But as we were small boys, two of the children would stand on the top of it and hold our hands to help us climb out. It was a very treacherous game. Some times the boys holding hands would leave them and the boy trying to come out will fall inside again. It was a good pastime.

Since the factory was in 50 acres of land the length from one gate to other was about ¾ km. In the evening we boys would run as fast as possible from one gate to the other. By 8 pm when we returned after playing we were so hungry that sometimes my mother was tired of cooking to feed us.

In the compound of our bungalow there were many fruit trees—like chikoo, maulshree, imli, goolar, ber, kabit and gonda. These fruits were entirely for us. We used to climb the trees and pluck these fruits and enjoy them.

In the year 1945 when I completed 5 years of age and began my 6th year I was admitted to a school run by Vinod Mills Ltd near Freeganj bridge. I was admitted in the first standard. At the time of admission my father mentioned my date of birth as 7th October 1939 and my name as Krishna Gopal Gupta. Earlier I was known as "Bangali" a name given by a Bengali nurse who attended my birth. I am more popular by the name of Bangali amongst my relatives, school and college friends in Ujjain.

This school had only three classes from 1st to 3rd standard. The distance was hardly 1 ½ km from my house. There was no traffic. People used to walk. Very few people used bicycles.

There was not a single car or scooter in the city of Ujjain. I used to walk alone with a cotton bag containing my books of Hindi and mathematics. School timings were from 11am to 4 pm. I would leave the house after lunch and return well within time to take afternoon snacks. There was only one teacher teaching us both subjects. Hindi was not difficult for me as it was my mother tongue. Maths was really a matter of suffering. Apart from numbers up to 100, tables were required to be crammed (tables of half, one and quarter and one and half to be remembered). Masterji always kept an elastic bamboo stick sufficiently oiled. He used to beat mercilessly for every fault in reciting tables. Now I think that in those days most of the teachers were sadists. They enjoyed beating small children. However this type of beating made the children thick skinned. Children would try several alibis to remain absent. My mother was so much for education that she would not listen to any plea for not going to school.

In the second standard, I was admitted to Madhavganj primary school. It was near my father's office. Timings were also suitable. I used to go to school with my father at 10 am. Father would leave me first in my school then go to his office. School would close at 4 pm. I would go to my father's office after school hours and return home with him. At that time no homework was given. To be very frank I did not like both these schools.

MY ELDEST SISTER SHAKUNTALA

My eldest sister Shakuntala was about 12 years elder to me. I was more attached to her than my mother. I used to eat and sleep with her. Without her I would not eat. She was my horse. Whenever we used to go to market I would walk a few steps and start crying that my legs were hurting. Out of love and affection for me, my sister would lift me up and carry me to the market and bring me back. I would always be waiting at the doorsteps for her return from school. As soon as I saw her coming I would run to meet her. She would lift me and bring me to the house. My mother would always say that his horse has come, why should he walk. She was also equally attached to me. She would always hang me in her lap and roam here and there doing her chores. Once my maternal uncle had come to live with us and during his stay I might have committed some misconduct. He was very much infuriated. It was common in those days to beat children. He started beating me with a stick. My sister saw all this. She came running and sprawled over me covering me fully. In the process she got five or six beatings but saved me from the rage of my maternal uncle. Due to the beating she suffered from ache and fever but saved me. She was married in 1947 when I was eight years old. This way I lost my good caretaker, sister cum mother and a good friend.

Daulatganj middle school

In the year 1948 I was admitted to Daulatganj Middle School in the 4th standard. It was a very good school. It was situated in the center of the city. It had a big playground. Adjacent to it was Madhav College, the only college in our city. College and our school shared a common boundary wall. Whenever there was a tournament of football, hockey or any other game we would jump over the wall to witness the tournament at college ground. I used to think that one day I too might get a chance to become a student of this college.

In Daulatganj middle school, I was admitted at the age of 9 years and left at the age of 13 years. I enjoyed my time in this school. I did not find any attraction in my earlier schools of Vinod Mills and Madhavganj therefore I often remained absent. But this was not the case with this school. I was always an hour early before the start of school. Sometimes my father was suspicious seeing me leave so early. Few times he came to school for a surprise check, but saw me playing on the ground.

In this school I developed a liking for football. Many would laugh if I say that we were playing real football. At that time there were no football shoes and for a ball we were having a tennis ball. Real football was given to us after school hours.

I have mentioned earlier that our school and college were having a common boundary wall. Near the boundary wall, there was the tennis court owned by the college. Often the ball would come into our school compound. At that time we eight or ten boys would be playing on our ground in the evening. Thus we would get sufficient balls for playing football before the school time and during recess.

MY TEACHERS

Teachers in this school were well qualified and devoted. I still remember the names of Radharaman Mehta our Hindi teacher and Dheer Saheb our science teacher. There were a few more who were having enormous love and affection for students.

I will be failing in my duty if I do not make a mention of our P.T Teacher, Shri Bhoite Sir. He was an ex-army man of Scindia state. A Maharashtrian gentleman of about 50 years of age. He was lean in body structure. In those days grounds were not properly laid out. There were lots of small pebbles on our ground. He would take us during the P.T. period and in the recess and tell us to collect pebbles. After the end of period or recess he will give 10 paisa to each of us from his own pocket. In those days purchasing power of 10 paisa was great. We enjoyed buying ground nuts and boiled grams for two or three days from the vendors sitting outside the gate of school.

When I reached 8th standard, I was selected for the school football team as well as Langdi game team. I passed middle board exam in the year 1952-53. At that time I was 13 years old.

GAMES AND ADVENTURES

I have mentioned earlier that I was staying in a bungalow situated in the center of a closed factory. There were ample opportunities for games. In summer vacation we used to play "Gulam Danda" game. In this game one person throws a stick from under his leg lifting it a little. One boy will run to collect it and in the mean time others will either hide or climb the trees. The boy, who collects the stick, would try to catch another boy. If he succeeded then the boy who was caught is declared out and he will have to collect the stick next time. Once, when one of the boys had thrown the stick it directly hit the eye of my elder brother. I had never seen so much blood in my life. All the boys were terrified. Many fled home. Few including me started crying with my elder brother. My father was in the office. My elder sister came running. I do not remember now how my brother was taken to the civil hospital. At that time there was no private hospital in Ujjain. Dr Khan was the eye surgeon. He treated my brother but could not save his eyesight. My brother permanently lost his eyesight. From that day we stopped playing that game.

There were two wells in the compound full of water. We used to take buckets and ropes and arrange a competition as to who will draw the maximum number of buckets, full of water, in 30 minutes. It was our regular game.

In the compound of ginning factory about 200 meters away from my bungalow was a pond full of clear water. We called it a Bawadi. It was 20'x20' in size. A tamarind tree was standing near it and a thick branch of that tree was running across the pond. In summer I along with other children would climb that branch to jump in that pond and enjoy its cool water. We could never fathom its depth.

Another adventure was to explore many closed sections of ginning factory. On the ground level of the factory there was a place for storing cotton bales. It was a closed shed. Above it was the main factory building accommodating various types of machines required for ginning cotton and making bales. All these machines were installed in a hall of approximate length and breadth of 50 by 50 meters. Here the cotton bales were prepared and pushed to a slide to send them to ground floor for stacking. In the hall there was an open hole where this slide was attached. The height of the slide was about 10 meters and width about 1 meter. We often climbed up this slide to the upper end and then slid to ground level. There was also a staircase leading to hall that was used by workers when the factory was in working condition. We were afraid to enter the hall either through the slide or staircase. Our parents in order to discourage us to undertake such an adventure had told us many stories in which snakes and ghosts were roaming freely in that factory hall. We assured our parents that we would keep a safe distance from the factory hall.

One day when we were playing on the slide one boy who was more courageous than others entered the main hall of factory building. He was always curious to know about this Hall. He started exploring it. Suddenly we heard a cry and the boy fell on the slide head down and started sliding with speed. Other boys were sitting on the slide. They stopped the momentum of his descent. The boy was senseless. One boy managed the emergency very well. He picked an empty tin container and brought sufficient water. He drenched the unconscious boy. The boy regained his consciousness but we could still notice that he was frightened. When he became normal we asked him the reason for his fear. He told us that he had seen an old man and woman eating a large snake. We discussed amongst us this matter for days but could not solve this mystery. However we never told our parents about this incident and decided that none of us would undertake such an adventure thereafter.

TEMPLE OF PALEBABA

About 100 meters from our house in the compound, there was a temple called "Palebaba Temple". No one knew when it was built. Someone told us that when the factory was under construction in the year 1875, one labourer died. He was a very saintly person. In his honour, the management built a temple. On several occasions we saw a snake inside the temple but it never harmed any one. We used to enter this temple many times without any fear. Surprisingly there were no snakebites during our stay of 15 years, though the entire area was a jungle and I had seen many big snakes. My sister Maya when writing her memories to assist me had written about this temple. Every Sunday she lit a "Deepak" in that temple. Once she forgot to light a deepak. Next day she saw a big snake. It happened two or three times whenever she forgot to light a deepak in temple of Palebaba. The temple is still in existence. I visited this temple recently in 2011.

During this time Dr. Khandekar was the civil surgeon of Ujjain civil hospital. He had one son of my age. He was the student of Devasgate middle school, which was near my school. The way to our school was the same. One day when I was walking to my school he met me on the way and we became friends. He invited my friends and I to play with him in the hospital compound. We stopped exploring the factory and started playing with him. Sometimes we would play, during full moon night, hide and seek game up to 10 pm at night. I have come to know that he is now settled in Indore and is a practicing doctor.

Arbi Ke Patte

Behind our bungalow there was a small pond created from our bathroom water. In this pond some "Arbi ke patte" had sprouted (commonly known as aloo ke pan). These are big leaves and used to prepare fried snacks liked very much by people from Maharashtra. Once when I visited the vegetable market I saw a boy selling these leaves. One Sunday I also collected about 100 leaves and reached the market. As soon as I entered a lady vendor saw me. She enquired of my intention. I told her that I would be selling these pan. She informed me that it would not be possible for me to do so as I should have permit to sit in the market. Observing disappointment on face she offered to purchase the entire lot. I cleverly considered it a good idea to sell it to her as it would save my time and no one known to me will notice sitting me selling such pan. She gave me one rupee and encouraged me to come again. I made it a routine once a month.

GULMOHAR TREE

There was a Gulmohar tree in the compound of our bungalow. A tree on which flowers blossom in summer. It becomes full of flowers. The color of the flowers of this tree is red and very attractive. Near my middle school there was a market of flower vendors called Malipura. I had to pass through this street to reach my school. One day I saw a heap of such flowers with a vendor. I inquired whether he would like to purchase if brought him some. He agreed subject to the quality of flowers. I noticed that water was sprinkled on flowers continuously. I was sure of the quality of my flowers. One Sunday I collected fresh flowers from the tree in a bed sheet and sprinkled water and carried to the Malipura. The person inspected the flowers and was very happy to purchase them. He paid me 12 annas. I accepted but made it clear to him that it will cost him one rupee next time if he wanted again. I had seen the face of other vendors who were observing flowers with interest and would be glad to pay me more. The vendor agreed and thus during summer I made five rupees. I made sufficient pocket money from these two businesses of mine.

IN BETWEEN 1953 AND 1955 THREE EVENTS TOOK PLACE

My father retired at the age of 55. Due to his disturbed life since his childhood and later carrying the burden of those who have earlier helped him, he could not accumulate any money. Thus my elder sister had to work and elder brother had to leave his studies. My elder sister Maya passed B.A. and was appointed as a teacher in Vijaya Raje Girls High school, a Government school, in which she had studied earlier.

My elder brother Narendra Kumar had to leave his education after completing Intermediate science to support the family. He joined post and telegraph department as a sorter, a very low position. He was a very intelligent person. Soon he passed departmental examination and was promoted to the position of Superintendent of post offices. He retired as the Assistant Postmaster General of M.P.

MAHARAJWARAH HIGH SCHOOL

In March 1953 I passed Middle Board Exam and sought admission in Maharajwarah High School. At that time there were only two high schools—one Maharajwarah and other one Model High School. Both were having co-education. One was at the south end of the city and other one was at the North end of the city. My school was near the famous "Mahankaleshwar Temple". It was the city palace for king Scindia but he never stayed there so it was converted into a school. It is said that he had enormous respect for king Vikramaditya who was the legendary king of Avantika (Ujjain). It was said that only the king superior to Vikramaditya in qualities could stay in Ujjain. Therefore as a mark of respect to king Vikramaditya, he decided to stay at the outskirt of the city and constructed his palace called Kaliadeh Palace at a distance of 15 km away from Ujjain on the riverbank of Shipra. River Shipra surrounds this palace from all the four sides. It was a beautiful sight and an enjoyable place for picnics.

The location of my school was very good. It was on a high ground. Within a radius of ½ km temples on the three sides and river Shipra on the other side surrounded it.

My school was about 4 km from my house. The school hours were from 10 am to 3 pm. I used to walk all the way to school and back. As I was interested in playing football I came back home after the school hours at 3 pm and after a glass of milk walked back to school play ground so as to be present there at 5 pm sharp. When I was a student of 9th standard, because of my earlier experience of playing football in middle school I was selected for the A-team of my high school. We practiced every day up to 6 to 7pm in summer. After practice I would walk back to my home. Thus every day I walked a minimum of 16 km.

My geography teacher, Shri Yeole Sahib, at that time was about 30 years of age and used to play with us in the position of full back. He encouraged us to be offensive with other teams. I played several matches on Madhav College ground when I was a student of Maharajwarah high school. The college sports teacher Shri Bhave used to arrange tournaments every year. Two teams that were A and B of college took part.

Teams from both the high schools, that is, Maharajwarah and Model school took part. Other teams like Railways sports club, Christian club and other teams from district also took part. This gave me a chance to become friendly with boys from the other college teams. When I took admission in the college in the year 1955 I did not face any difficulty as many star players of the college knew me and they welcomed me and supported me on every occasion.

Yeole sahib would always play with us. He was a very good person and loved the players so much that he arranged refreshments for us many time after practice hours, all from his meager salary. In school he would support us even if any of us had committed any misconduct. He used to argue our case before the Head Master. He arranged a white half pant and blue silk shirt as the school football team uniform for us. Sometimes we used to wear this uniform during regular school just to impress others.

My school Maharajwarah was near the temple of Mahankaleshwar. I was lucky to have chosen this school for Matriculation. I had darshan practically every day. Whenever there was a free period (a period when no teacher comes to teach) I would go to the old temple of Mahankaleshwar and sit there. If you go for the darshan of Mahankaleshwer during your Ujjain visit please do visit the old temple and sit there for some time. You will experience enormous peace. It is in the same compound behind the new temple. Very few outsiders know about this temple. You will be able to sit and pray undisturbed and no one will be there to tell you to move.

MY SECOND ELDER SISTER MAYA

When I was in the 9th standard my elder sister Maya was pursuing her studies of M.A.(Hindi) in Madhav College the only college of the city. She used to bring many literary books from the college library. My father was also an ardent reader of Hindi novels. He was a member of Yuvraj General Library. There were about 60,000 books on different subjects in that Library at that time. One day I started reading Kamayani of Jaishankar Prasad. My sister told me not to read such difficult book but advised me to start with short stories and suggested stories by Premchand. I read all the seven parts of Manasarovar a collection of short stories by Premchandji. Later during the next three years I read almost all the good works of prominent writers of Hindi like Premchand, Gurudutta, Acharya Chatursen Shastri, Rahul Sanskritayan, Bhagvaticharan Varma, Vindavanlal Varma, Bhartendu Harishchandra, Kabir, Rahim, Kalidas, Raskhan, Surdas, Tulsidas, Jaishankar Prasad, Niraala, Pant, Mahadevi Varma, Dinkar, Phanishwarnath Renu, Maithalisaran Gupt and many other. I read Indumati a novel, written by Seth Govindas comprising of 900 pages, in just two days.

I also read Bengali and Marathi writers work translated into Hindi. Prominent amongst them were Gurudeo Tagore, Sharatchandra, Bamkimchandra, Bimal Mitra, Taracand Bandhpadyay, Narendranath Mitra, Bhausaheb Khandekar and many others.

End of golden period of my life

When I was in the 10th standard, the owner sold the factory. My family had to move out. The purchaser started dismantling the machinery. Land was to be handed over to the Civil Hospital authorities.

My golden period of life ended. Slogans like 'life is beautiful' vanished in clouds unexpectedly. We moved to the old city of Ujjain. Our new house had only two rooms and a kitchen, on the first floor of a building. No land for gardening and only houses after houses having a common wall. I did not like the environment. We were 6 brothers and sisters. Total eight persons with mother and father. I started passing time either in the old temple or other places where I could feel near nature. I passed Matriculation exam in March 1955. At that time my age was 15 years.

I had learnt to ride a bicycle. I was exploring the city with one or two friends the entire day. We would start after breakfast, take a pack of lunch with us and explore the outskirts of the city.

SINHASAN OF VIKRAMADITYA

Just behind Mahakalshwar Mandir there is a small hill. It was said that it was there that Vikramaditya's seat (Sinhasan) was buried. There is a popular story about this seat of the king Vikramaditya. One day a herds-boy went there with his cows and sat on that hill. He started giving verdicts like a king. Many people from the city went there with their grievances and he solved them judiciously. He carried on for many days and after that the Sinhasan was taken away by the caretakers (putlis) of king Vikramaditya into the sky.

As boys, we also heard this story and often went to the hill to play and pray there. Few boys and girls of my class and other classes also visited and requested to fulfill their wishes, mostly about passing the exam. Their wishes were granted.

Recently I met one of my classmates in Ujjain. He was with his wife Usha, who was also a student of 10th class. I was surprised and asked him when did he marry her. He laughed and said that it was the result of their wish at the hill.

The hill still exists there. You can see from the backside of the old temple of Mahankaleshwar or if you take a guide he will certainly show you the place.

HARSIDDHI DEVI TEMPLE

Next to this hill there is a temple known as "Harsiddhi Devi Temple". Harsiddhi means a goddess who fulfills all the wishes. The way to the temple is from Mahankaleshwar. A small road goes to this temple. The distance from Mahankaleshwar is hardly half a kilometer. On both the sides of this road there is a lake, which is mostly full of water and excess rainwater flows to River Shipra that flows behind this temple.

This temple has a big courtyard in which two round pillars stand. The height of these two pillars is about 30 feet and diameter about 10 feet at the base and 4 feet at the top. All around these pillars a hallow space is provided to hold the "deepaks". During Navratri festival deepaks full of oil are put at these places and people light them. Thousands of deepak are put at these two pillars. Many people come to have darshan of this Goddess during Navratri and see this festival of lights.

As boys, we would visit this play everyday in groups. It was like a small fair. At that time Ujjain was a small city with a population of hardly 50,000.

Here during such a festival I was attracted to a girl. Her father was at that time a Doctor in Civil Hospital of Ujjain. She was also a student of my school. Her name was Sumitra which created confusion later when my father fixed my marriage in

1966 and sent a photo to me. It was an attraction every boy has towards girls in adolescence age. It was nothing serious.

Both of us passed the 10th standard and took admission in Madhav College, the only college at that time in Ujjain. She became the student of Arts faculty and I was in commerce. Our Timings were different. We seldom met. Later her father was transferred and she left college and the city as well. When we were married I found for sure that she was the same girl the daughter of the doctor. But it was my mistake. Any way it was a blessing in disguise. She of course did not remember me as the girls generally do not pay attention to their schoolmates. When I told her about our school and college she did not remember.

I think God is very kind to me because of my frequent visits to Mahankaleshwar during our free periods. In my life I have experienced four times that some invisible power has helped me. About this I will write at a proper time.

In the courtyard of Harsiddhi Devi temple there is one room sealed by the Government. When I was 5 years old I visited this place with my father for the first time to witness the festival of lights. I saw the room and when I inquired I was told that there is one tunnel, which goes to Bhartari cave which is 10km away from this temple. In this cave Raja Bhartari did meditation for many years. As a child I was thrilled and curious to know more about this tunnel. I asked many question as to why it was sealed. My father told me that one person tried to go to the cave through this tunnel but neither reached the cave nor came back. In this tunnel now many old saints are doing meditation along with saint Bhartari and they do not want any disturbance. I was thrilled and that night I saw myself walking in to that tunnel but was frightened and my mother sat whole night with me to calm me.

Later after many years, I took both my sons there. The guide told them the same story about that room. They were also thrilled and curious. No one is interested in knowing the facts. Everyone is only interested in passing on this story generation after generation to thrill their children. If you happen to visit you will be shown this room and the same story will be retold. I am sure your kids will enjoy it.

RIVER SHIPRA

Down the temple if you walk for about half a kilometer you will find river Shipra flowing and you will reach Ramghat. The river is the most sacred river after Narmada. This is the river on the bank of which Simhastu (Kumbh) fair takes place after every 12 years. In India this fair is organized at four places viz Haridwar, Allahabad, Nasik and Ujjain.

I learnt to swim in this river. The river is 300 feet wide. This is the river where all the children of Ujjain learn to swim. During summer vacation all the children would come early morning to the river. Many people would bring sealed containers, car and truck tubes and wooden planks. Children learn swimming with the help of these items. Many Pahalwan (wrestlers) who came for massage by their Chelas would keep a watch on us. Upstream of the river about one km there is a ghat called Narshing Ghat. Many children after acquiring some skill were allowed to swim from Ramghat to Narshingh Ghat. But it was necessary for them to take containers and tubes with them in case of need.

Many swimmers used to surround us while swimming to Narsingh Ghat. It was a fantastic sight to see the river full of many swimmers in the river with tin containers and tubes. We would enjoy for almost two hours. After finishing our swimming exercise we were given Jilebis by elderly rich people who were visiting the river every day. Many stalls for Jilebi and samosas were put up and these seth (rich elderly people) were happy to call the children and give them one samosa and four Jilebis. A visit to river Shipra is a must. Without it Ujjain pilgrimage is incomplete. The river has well built ghats covering its entire length of three kilometer through the city.

DUTT KA AKHARA

Just opposite to Ramghat on the river Shipra there is one muth called "Dutt ka Akhara". It was the place for lodging and boarding of saints visiting Ujjain. All the facilities were provided free of cost. Expenses were borne by Gwalior State, out of the funds from Gangajali. It was a fund created from the tax collected from Ujjain city. The total revenue collection was deposited in this fund and State was not authorized to spend the amount on anything else, except for the development of Ujjain, as it was the holy city of Scindia State.

One saint, who was Gaddinashin (Mahant) at that time, was very holy and famous. As a Prasad he distributed Seera (Haluwa) made from wheat flour, sugar and pure ghee. The quantity distributed at a time to one person was approximately 100 to 200 grams given in a Dona (cup made of leafs).

My house was approximately 1.5 km from this Akhara. I, with other children would visit daily in the hope of getting Seera. Every day after coming from school at about 4 pm it was our daily routine to visit this Akhara. Sometimes we went twice to take the prasad. Mahant, though knowing this fact often obliged us with a smile.

My mother was worried as to why I was not eating anything in the afternoon after coming from school. Eating 100 to 200 gm seera daily made of pure ghee and sugar resulted in increase of my weight. One day my father looked at me and told my mother to reduce my diet. My mother immediately came to my rescue and informed father that I was not eating even afternoon meals and asked how the boy could gain weight. She advised father to go for an eye test. On that day I realized how much a mother loves her children. However fearing that father might inquire further I stopped going to the Akhara but the urge for Seera was so strong that it forced me to visit the place twice a week.

The Mahant was a saint in the real sense. Once it so happened that the stock of ghee was finished. Everyone was worried how the Prasad will be prepared. Mahant prayed to the Dutt God the main deity of the Akhara. Suddenly he took a bucket and went to river and came back with a bucket full of water. He told the other saints to put this water of river Shipra and cook the Prasad. Everyone thought that the Mahant has lost his sense because of the shock, as it was the first time he was not able to provide ghee for Prasad. But to every ones' surprise water turned into ghee. The next day the Mahant received the ghee and took one bucket full of ghee, went to river and poured it in the river. The ghee went down immediately. Mahant departed to heaven within a week's time. Later I heard that Mahant had taken ghee from Holy River on the promise of returning it the next day. I visited again recently. Now no Prasad is being distributed but the memories are still alive. The feeling of that Mahant is still there. Those who had seen those days still visit this place. One must visit this Datt ka Akhara during his visit to Ujjain.

Sandipani Ashram

On the outskirts of my town Ujjain about 3 km is Sandipani Ashram. This is the Ashram where Krishna and Sudama were taught by the Rishi Sandipani.

The Ashram still gives a feeling of the fragrance of Rishi. It has a pond in the center. There is only one hut. It must have been dense forest there at the time of Krishna and Sudama.

Here I realized that the aim of education is not to make a man rich. Sudama was well educated but never used his ability to earn money. It is for the all round development of all your faculties. To make you more sensitive to the problems of the society. In our young age we are at the receiving end from the society. We should always repay it. During that visit I became more emotional. I had a feeling that someone was guiding me for future and telling me how to shape my life.

GARH KI KALIKA

This is a Kali Devi Mandir. It is called 'Garh ki' because it resembles a fortress in nature. It has a high parapet walls. Inside these walls is a small ground and at the end of the ground there is temple of Kalika. Who constructed this temple is not known. The inscription there says, that it is 400 years old. There must have been a dense forest here at that time.

When I was 12 years old, I visited this temple with my school friends. Then it was also a forest area and our parents forbade us to go there alone. There were many Ber trees. (I don't know the exact English word for this fruit). We, a few children of same age used to go there with our lunch boxes, in the greed of collecting Ber and enjoying the afternoon. Once, seven or eight of us had gone there and were collecting Ber and also climbing the trees and in this process were destroying the fruits. One girl sitting on a machan in her tomato field saw us and threw a pebble from her sling. It so happened that the pebble struck the head of a boy and he began to bleed. Now I think it was just like a scene shown in many movies where the heroine throws a stone that strikes the hero, and then she comes to bandage the hero. Here the difference was that her mother came and took all of us to her house. She put some turmeric and bandaged the wound. She offered all of us hot milk and gave us Ber. She also scolded the girl. I still remember the name of that lady, Parwati and girl Shyamla.

Recently when I visited this temple I visited their house. Parwati is no more. Her son was there. Shyamla is married and lives in some other village. When I narrated the incident, he offered me and my wife a cup of tea. Now there are no more Ber trees.

TEMPLE OF BHAIRAVBABA

Very near Garh Ki Kalika is a temple of Bhairavnath. It is famous for offering of liquor as a Prasad. Approximately 1000 bottles are offered every day now. Near the boundary wall of this temple the river Shipra flows. In spite of so much offering of liquor no trace is visible around the temple or in the river. I visited it now in the year 2009 during one of my visits to Ujjain with few friends from Nasik. In those days of my childhood it was a dense forest area and children were prohibited to visit that place.

CAVE OF RAJA BHARTARI

Here king Bhartari meditated for 14 years with his guru sitting on his shoulders. King Bhartari was the king of Ujjain in the sixth century. He renounced his kingdom and gave the reins to his younger brother Vikramaditya. It is an underground cave having four large rooms, now kept very tidy. This underground cave is further down to 1.2 km from Garh Ki Kalika temple on the bank of river Shipra. There are two tunnels inside the cave, one is incoming on the west side and another one going out from east side. Incoming one is coming from Harsiddhi Temple that I have already mentioned, while I wrote about Harsiddhi. Other one that is going out, it is said that it goes to Banaras. Both are now closed by the Archeological Department. I never believed these but tourist are still being told this story.

When I was a student of 10th standard, I had visited this cave many times with my friends. We thought the east side tunnel must be leading to the river to facilitate the king Bharthari to go for a bath in the river. We searched the bank of the river many kilometers but could not find an opening. We often visited this place. The Sadhus were very affectionate and often offered us Dal Batti (A famous meal of Malwa. Ujjain is in Malwa region) We used to go there and swim in the river. At that time the river had flowing water and was waist deep from one bank to other. We would take out all our clothes and swim naked in the river as this was a secluded area. We carried no towels.

We would dry ourselves in hot sun. At that time there were no cameras available otherwise I would certainly have taken my photo and kept it in my album so that my great grand children would feel proud how advanced their Dadaji was, taking a sunbath in those times. One should visit this cave whenever one happens to visit Ujjain.

Madhav College Ujjain

In the year March 1955 I appeared for Matriculation examination and passed it in second division. I filled the form for admission for intermediate course in Madhav College. I opted for commerce subjects. In those days getting admission was not a problem. My college timings were from 7 am to 11 am. The first day was an emotional day for me. My dream had come true. Earlier I had mentioned that when I was in Daulatganj Middle School I was often thought as to whether I would get a chance to become the student of this college. The day had dawned now and my dream had come true.

It was not a hard day for me. Many students of Model school who had also taken admission were my good friends though they were fierce opponents on the football ground. Many senior students of Madhav College who were football players were also known to me. They were good boys and friendly therefore I did not feel that I had come to some new place. I completed two years of intermediate course without any event worth mentioning except that I took part in games and was class representative.

SATIN DESAI, O.P. KAUSHIK AND THE FINAL MATCH OF FOOTBALL THAT I WILL NEVER FORGET

Every year shree N.R.Bhave sir our sports teacher used to arrange Football tournament. If I remember correctly it was in the year 1956, sometimes in the month of August or September he arranged a tournament to be played on a league basis. In such a tournament every team plays with each of the participating team and the two teams that score the highest points play in the finals. Many teams took part. Matches were played continuously for fifteen days. Our captain was Satin Desai. He was an extraordinary player not just of football but many other games equally well. He could not take part in this tournament. He was stabbed by some antisocial elements for reason best known to them. He was admitted in the Civil Hospital which was close to our college.

Our team had reached up to the final. O.P.Kaushik was playing as the Goal Keeper. It was said about him that if O.P is playing as a goalkeeper, the ball is afraid of entering the goal. Other team playing in final against us got many opportunities to put the ball in goal but O.P proved their attempts futile. In those days he was the best goalkeeper of Ujjain District and all the affiliated colleges of our university.

Civil Hospital authorities had made special arrangements for Satin to see the match. His sitting arrangement was made on the terrace of the Hospital Staff quarter. From this terrace college ground was clearly visible. In between this quarter and college ground there was a boundary wall, along a small road. There was a gate in the boundary wall of college ground to reach this road.

The game started. Satin was watching the play. Both the teams were playing with their full might. Spectators too were cheering the players of their team and shouting encouraging words. There was great uproar from all the four sides of the ground. It was 90 minutes play. Just before the end of match we scored one goal. I do not remember now who scored it. As soon as the whistle was blown signaling the end of the game, all of us players ran to meet Satin. We crossed the road and reached the terrace. He was happy but looking pale from the fatigue of sitting for 90 minutes. I remember that he was smiling. That was our best gift to our Captain. He was not allowed to enjoy our victory for some more time, because soon hospital authorities moved him to his room.

Later at the function of price distribution every one said that we won because of O.P. Memories of that match have a thrilling impact on me even now.

NATIONAL CADET CORPS

In those days, NCC training had been made optional in every college. On each Sunday morning, for two to three hours we had to undergo several exercises. After parade sumptuous refreshments were given. Every year two Khaki dresses, one pair of boot were given. During the training I learnt how to keep boots and belt shining. I always attended Sunday parade with great interest. I also attended two training camps.

1. from 25.12.1955 to 7.1.1956 at Nazarpur

2. from 22.12.1956 to 4.1.1957 at Bercha

I attended one social service camp too from 15.5.1956 to 28.5.1956 at Tajpur. In this camp I learned about community living. In all these camps cadets from 8 to 10 colleges numbering approximately 600 attended.

It was a great experience of living in tents. For the first time I realized how a soldier is trained through strenuous and comprehensive training. In a camp we used to get up at 5 am. It was quite chilly in December and January that too in a remote area where camps were always held. The whole day up to 5 pm exercise, parade and classes were conducted except for one hour lunch break. In evening attendance in games was compulsory. Dinner time was from 7.30 to 8.30

pm. There after campfire used to be arranged, where cadets come in contact with each other and a bond of friendship developed amongst the students of different colleges.

By 10.30 pm we were stone tired and slept like a dead log.

I passed intermediate final examination in 1957 in second division as usual.

MY FRIEND
MANGILAL GUPTA

When I took admission in the 1st year commerce in Madhav College I met a boy. He had done matriculation from Model High School. He was in my class. He was living a furlong away from my house. As our timings of class were the same we walked together to the college. He became my staunch supporter. He supported me in every activity. He canvassed vigorously in elections for me. He was good at studies. We exchanged notes. When I was suspended from college for seven days he too did not attend the college. When I took a drop in 1959 he too did not appear for examination. When I again took admission after returning from Indore he too joined the college. Both of us passed M. Com. together. His father was in cotton trade. His mother treated me as her son. Many times I ate at his home and vice versa. He was married when he was still a student. Later we became family friends. He again completed M.A in sociology and became lecturer in Madhav College itself. His son who is in Mumbai is a very senior corporate executive and is still maintains family relations with me. He has two children and they often come to stay with me. Mangilal died in the year 1993 due to sudden heart attack. He was 54 years of age. Thus I lost a very good friend.

My college union activities

In the year 1957 I took admission in the first year of two years course of B.Com. Apart from sports activities I took part in extracurricular activities of college. I was a class representative. I was also elected as Secretary of Commerce Association during 1957-1958. It was a tough fight. Against me a student of B.com. final year was contesting. I got 11 votes and he got 10 votes I was declared the winner. During this election I came in contact with Shri Devichand Sharma known by many names like Ustad and Adalat.

He helped me in winning the election. He contacted all the class representatives and canvassed for me.

He was senior to me but an active worker in all the fields of college activities and very popular amongst students. I was a member of student federation but it had nothing to do with communist party.

In the Final year 1958-1959, I was elected as Secretary of Vidhyarthi Sahayak Sabha without any visible opposition.

MY ACT OF THEFT

In the year 1958-1959, a photograph of Madhav College Ujjain Football team of Vikram University champions was arranged. Everyone had to pay Rs 10/-. At that time I was not having this amount. I did not have the courage to ask to my father. My other sources of income—Arbi ke patte and Gulmohar flowers—was no more available to me. My elder sister Maya was at that time the Head mistress of Madhavnagar Middle school. In her purse she always had some money. I took Rs 10 without informing her. The Money was to be paid by me for a copy of photograph to be taken in the evening. After some time my conscience reproached me. I put back that amount in her purse. However college authorities were kind enough to print my name on the photograph though I was absent.

MY SUSPENSION FROM COLLEGE

During this year I along with one of my friend, suspended from college for 7 days. No reason was given. As soon as the notice was displayed both of us became heroes. Fellow students started looking at us with unspoken honour. I did not have the courage to see the principal and ask the reason. After some time I came to know that during half yearly exam someone had rubbed the juice from a stick on the table of a fellow girl student. The juice causes an itch when it comes in comes in contact with the skin. The juice had dried and she could not give terminal exam due to itch. The stick was known as 'Kainch ki fali'. On her complaint, though she did not mention our name, I and the other boy were suspended because my seat was just behind her.

However we were only suspended and given the benefit of doubt. At that time I did not realize the seriousness of the incident, but somewhere in my subconscious mind this was stored. Whenever I remembered this it pained me. I decided that if given a chance I would certainly clarify the matter to that girl student. In the year 1988 when I was working as the General Manager of a Paper mills near Bhusawal, I often visited Ujjain. During one of such visits I traced that girl. I met her and explained the purpose of my visit. The first impression I got was that she looked amazed but soon recovered and laughed. She remembered the incident. I told her that I was not the culprit and was carrying this burden on my soul for a very long time. I just wanted to clarify the matter before her so that I am relieved burden of a sin that I had not committed. She took it in a good sense of humour and assured me, though she remembers the incident, but had forgotten me and my friend. On that day the stain of uncommitted sin was washed from my soul.

In the month of March 1959 I appeared for B.Com Final examination and passed it with a second Division.

EMPLOYEES STATE INSURANCE CORPORATION (ESIC)

In the month of May 1959 there was a position vacant in ESI Corporation of India. I applied, appeared for the written examination and was appointed as a clerk in the Regional Office of the Corporation in Indore a city 60 km away from Ujjain. My father did not agree. He advised me first to complete my education. I assured him that I would take the admission in Holkar College Indore and continue my education.

MR. BHARGAVA
A KIND GENTLEMAN

I Joined ESI Corporation and took admission in Holkar College, Indore. The college timings were 7.30 am to 11am and office was from 10am to 6pm. At that time my basic salary was Rs. 150 and DA of Rs. 15 thus total salary was Rs.165. Mr. Bhargava was the office Superintendent. He was about 50 years of age and a kind gentleman. He adjusted my office timings. He gave me the table of dispatch clerk requiring my presence from 11 am to 7 pm. Though I used to come directly from college but could not make before 11 am. My other colleagues managed my work. Since my main object was to complete my education I was not paying proper attention to my work. I often made mistakes. Post, which was to be dispatched to Raipur, was dispatched to Jabalpur and so on. Mr. Bhargava received letters of complaint from Managers of local offices of Raipur, Jabalpur, Bhopal and other district places but he ignored and never put those before Regional Director. He said that when you work, mistakes occur, mistakes are meant to be committed; therefore the door for correction is always open. He loved all the youngsters like his son. Here for the first time I realized that everywhere one can find good people, ready to help provided, one is sincere.

REGIONAL DIRECTOR MR. A.N. BIDANI

I was also greatly impressed by Mr. A.N. Bidani, a Punjabi gentlemen who was the Regional Director of M.P. Region. He used to attend office always an hour earlier than the scheduled time and would leave only after completing his work. Any file submitted for his decision would return within half an hour. I remember an incident that one day a file was not traceable. Somebody suggested searching it in the chamber of Mr. Bidani. It had been submitted for his approval a day before. Superintendent out right rejected the idea arguing that he will never keep the file with him. The file was found in our office later.

Mr. Bidani, was so devoted to his work that whenever he returned from tour even at 4pm, he came to office directly from the railway station. His way of working made a great impression on me. I learnt that only hard working and sincere persons could come up in life and achieve their goal. I decided to work hard in future and remain sincere in my work.

However the pressure of office work and studies resulted in unmanageable fatigue and I could not prepare myself for exam. Though I could have passed the exam but my object was to clear it with a first class. I did not appear for the examination. I was worried what would I say to my father. One day I was sitting sadly in the office. It so happened that Mr. Bidani unexpectedly came on his round. He sensed that something was wrong with me. He called me in his office. I narrated him my story. He did not say a thing. Perhaps he understood my difficulties and burning desire for higher studies. I remember it was a Friday. Next Monday I received my transfer order to Ujjain office-my hometown—with a simple note of his Ashirvad. Here my conviction got strength that everywhere there are good people provided you are sincere. Secondly I realized that God is kind to me as he always keeps me in company of good people. I had the perception of his kindness, as this was a clear proof.

MR. R.R.MISHRA
MANAGER LOCAL OFFICE OF
E.S.I. CORPORATION UJJAIN

Mr Mishra was a young man of about 35 years of age. He was a sportsman who liked to play volleyball. One day he called me to his office. He knew that I was also a sportsman. He asked me if it would be possible for him to play volleyball at college court with students. I discussed the matter with Shri N.R.Bhave, the sports teacher and introduced Mr. Mishra to him. He welcomed Mr. Mishra and allowed him to play at the college ground. He started playing volleyball on every Saturday and Sunday. In summer he would see that office is closed sharp at 5 pm so that he could reach in time to play at college ground. He would always take me with him on his scooter. He had been granting me leave for preparation for 45 days before my examination. He would whenever occasion arrived advise me that the job of ESI Corporation was not fit for me. I must make teaching as my career. I agreed with him and after passing my M.Com examination I resigned from the services of E.S.I.Corporation of India.

Back to my old College

In July 1960 I took admission in Madhav College Ujjain again to complete my studies. I had taken admission in M.Com. part one.

All my old friends welcomed me, though they had become seniors but never gave me this impression. I attended office and college regularly. I had to say goodbye to my sports and extracurricular activities. Even then I was invited to attend all the activities due to my past association.

In the year 1962, I successfully completed my M.Com. Exam but could not secure first class. I secured 298 marks out of 500 and lost 1st class by just two marks. I was expecting 80 marks in Statistics but got just 45 marks. I applied for rechecking. At that time rechecking meant re-totaling. My uncle who was Asst Registrar in University advised me not to press the issue further. Later I came to know the reason. I was not in good books of a professor due to my union activities. He examined answer sheets of this subject. He deliberately undervalued it. I did not believe this on the contrary, I said if such was the case I should remain thankful to him for giving me 45 marks otherwise he could have declared me fail and could have spoiled my future. This way I completed my education. Simultaneously I resigned from ESI Corporation service.

In 1962 Government of Madhya Pradesh had undertaken massive expansion of Higher secondary schools. Schools were opened in every village. I was appointed as a commerce teacher in higher secondary school Namli a village 10km away from Ratlam a district place. The Principal Mr. Munshi was the Head Master when I was student of Maharajwada. He saw his own signature on my school leaving certificate and was very happy with me. I did not face any problem.

LIFE IN NAMLI

In those days Namli was a very small village having about 100 houses. In the radius of about 5 to 7 km, many small villages surrounded it. Therefore Government had opened a Higher Secondary school at this place. It had a railway station. A meter gauge train was running from Ratlam to Chittor and Ajmer. I rented a house of a Patwari. It was quite a spacious house having a well inside for daily need for water. The rent was only Rs 10 a month. My school hours were from 10 am to 3 pm. I had sufficient time to cook in the morning and evening. My mother had taught me to cook two or three dishes.

In the evenings we played volleyball on the village volleyball ground. I was tolerably well in playing many games including volleyball. Patwari himself liked to play. Thakur of Namli who was 40 years of age and his younger brother who was of my age also played this game with us alongwith the police inspector of village police station. Every day we would play from 5 to 7 pm. Life was easy in those days.

Thakur of Namli was having a palatial house surrounded by forests and his agricultural land. Once he hosted a dinner. His younger brother who was friendly with me invited me. First I hesitated but on his persuasion I agreed. Every one assembled at about 8 pm. There were about 100 people from nearby villages mostly Thakurs who were landlords before

1950. They mostly talked about their grandeur of olden days. Few were young friends of the younger Thakur. We sat in a separate group. Drinks were served.

A few of the youngsters including me had not opted for drinks. Snacks both veg and mostly non-veg were served. Younger thakur explained that the liquor being served was made 60 year before, at the time of his grandfather. It was called Kesar Kasturi. His grandfather employed an expert in brewing liquor. He showed me the cellar of his palace where hundreds of bottles were kept in a systematic way. After 11 pm, dinner was served. It was very rich food full of spices and ghee. The cook was well trained and had travelled whole of Europe with Thakur. In those days Europe was a much favoured destination of Indian Landlords and kings. USA was not so popular. The Cook was expert in cooking various dishes.

The party ended by 12 pm. A few of them went to the forest for hunting. I do not know when they returned. I came back to my residence by 1 am. I still remember that party.

SAILANA

As I have written that small and big Thikanas surrounded Namli, where fortresses (commonly known as Garhi) of landlords can still be seen. One of such places was Sailana about 10 km from Namli.

Sailana was bigger than Namli. Thakur saheb of Sailana was having a big fortress surrounded by high walls all the four sides. Inside the wall a big ground was there which could easily accommodate 5,000 people. It had two gates, one for daily use, which was smaller and other gate, opened on the occasion of special celebrations, and was very big, through which an elephant can pass easily. He celebrated Teej every year. It is very important festival in Malwa. Ladies would sow wheat in a utensil and on tenth day when wheat called jawara sprouted and attains height of 12 inches they celebrate the festival. On that day the big gate was opened for public. Many people assembled to see the function. Men and women performed different type of dances.

During my stay in Namli I happened to get a chance to witness such celebration. Our group of 10 to 12 persons had gone in a jeep of Police Inspector. In those days tar roads were not joining every village. The kachha road passed through the forest. We started at 5pm and reached there by 6pm. The program started by sun set. It was almost 3 hours spell binding program. We returned in night through forest area but those days law and order position was good and the police inspector was with us therefore no one was afraid.

A BOY WHO OFTEN COMES IN MY DREAM

In class 9th of which I was a class teacher there was a boy who used to come from one of the nearby villages. He was a son of the erstwhile landlord, a Thakur. He had passed 8th class from his village school. The boy was very attractive. He always wore a smile on his face. But if seen carefully one could have easily spotted a hidden anguish behind that smile. He was suffering from polio below hips. He used to come on a horse driven TONGA or on the back seat of a bicycle with his servant. One person was always with him to lift and carry him. I had made special arrangements for him to sit and watch other boys playing at school ground. Whenever I saw him sitting I tried to understand how he would be feeling watching other boys of his age playing when he could not even stand. That day I realized that God is kind to us who have no physical disability. He was very intelligent. He wanted some lesson in Accountancy. I had gone to his Garih (a small fortress). I met his mother and father who were still giving impression of an aristocratic race but were heavy hearted due to the sufferings of their son. Next year he passed matriculation board examination with good marks. At that time I was in Ratlam. His father sent a message requesting me to come to his village as his son wanted to see me. I purposely did not go there as it was unbearable for me to see suffering of such a charming boy.

I have already written that I could play many games tolerably well. In those days cricket was not so popular. In villages volleyball was more popular. Every Sunday I was called in one or other village either to play or to work as umpire. This gave me a chance to see the life of villagers who were living in isolated places. I also saw the life of erstwhile landlords. They were unable to maintain their fortresses. Though they were having enough land but they had never worked with their own hands. It was difficult for them to maintain their life style.

OPIUM FIELDS

Namli and surrounding area are famous for their opium fields. I visited these fields first time. The sight attracted not only me but also all of my friends who had come to meet me from Ujjain. In a field one can see different colour of flowers like white, red, blue, green and yellow. It was mesmerizing sight. An elderly person in our group said, "even a beautiful thing if not put to proper use may cause so much suffering to the world as opium does".

MY TRANSFER TO DISTRICT SCHOOL AND SUNEEL WILLIAM

In the year 1963 due to my sincerity and good result I was transferred to District school of Ratlam. The school was in the center of the city called Manakchowk. Principal was Mr Gokhru. He was a sportsman. I was very happy. Life was easy. Apart from teaching commerce subjects I was appointed as the coach of Football team.

Suneel William was a student of 9th class. I was the class teacher. He had good control of a Football. In every respect he was a good Football player. But during selection matches selection committee member did not select him as he was short in height. He was below 5 feet. As I was the coach and one of the members of selection committee too, I insisted that he should be included in the team. Selection Committee members agreed to take him as extra player with a promise from me that I will not give him chance to play in main team unless some emergency occurred. We started for Ujjain to participate in inter district Football tournament. About 40 teams took part. My school played its first match. Though many opportunities were there but our strikers could not steer the ball into goal. The match resulted in a draw. Extra time of 15 minutes was given to play. I replaced one of the players and substituted Suneel in the forward line. Players of opposite team laughed and nicknamed him "Dwarf". He got a chance.

He received the ball, controlled it, dodged three of the players and kicked the ball with precision in the corner of the goal. We won the match. Thereafter this boy became the center of attraction. He played so well during all the matches that our team reached in the Finals. Principal Mr Gokhru came to Ujjain to witness the final match. My team won the match and the trophy. Suneel William was later selected to represent the State. This was a great honour to this school. Principal was so pleased that he sent an extraordinary report about me. He called me in his office and showed it to me. I was expecting a promotion. But God had something else in store for me. I was selected for training with full pay in Regional College of Education Bhopal the capital city of Madhya Pradesh.

TERMINATION OF MY SERVICES

While I was in training the orders for terminating my services were served on me. Every one of my colleagues was surprised. Principal Mr. Gokhru visited Bhopal to represent my case but without any success. Later I came to know that it was because of my union activities. I was the member of Student Federation that was considered as the student body of communist party. It was Government policy not to give employment to communists. Student Federation of our college was not affiliated to Communist party. I hardly knew about communism. With me many more people's services were terminated. One was lecturer in a Government college and another was police inspector. I do not know about others. Later they had gone to court and after three years were reinstated with full salary.

I left my training course and returned to Ujjain as an unemployed youth. I had come to square one standing on the cross roads where from I had started. Now the only difference was that I did not know which road to walk. I often asked God why he did such thing with me. Many years later when I had settled well I thought that had my services were not terminated I would never have left the teaching job.

My Friend
Shri Narendra Jain

One of my classmates was Shri Narendra Jain. He was an Income Tax Sales Tax practitioner. He wanted to open a office in Dewas a district place about 30 km away from Ujjain. He proposed that I should take two months training in his office and then take independent charge of Dewas Office. It was an attractive proposal but I do not know why I declined. Both of us were good friends and used to go for morning walk together. I was so much devoted to the teaching job that many a times I told him that I would run a school. The students will have a dress code (at that time dress code was not there). I used to talk like a conventional fool (sheikhchilli). Without even having 100 rupees in my pocket I was dreaming of having my own school. He used to laugh and advised me to find a job first.

My friend
Babu Maheshwari

My friend Shri Krishnakant Bangur, known as Babu Maheshwari was a nice person. His father Shri C.L.Maheshwari was chief executive of West Coast Paper Mills in Dandeli, Karnataka. Babu sent my application to his father who forwarded it to his Bombay office. It was a combined office. Somanis, who were at that time partners with Bangurs sat together in this office. It was called Shriniwas house and was situated behind Bombay Gymkhana in Fort area. Somanis had their own personal factories too. I received a call for an interview. I interviewed and was offered a job in Accounts Department of a partnership firm known as Oriental Can Manufacturing Company. I joined this firm on 4th December 1964. Thus my unemployment ended. I had to see what God had now destined me to receive. The year 1964 ended here for me.

End of my life story from 1939 to 1964

PART TWO

MY LIFE STORY
FROM 1965 TO 1980

ARRIVAL IN BOMBAY

It was my first visit to the city of Bombay. I reached Bombay on 3rd of December 1964. I only had two hundred Rupees in my pocket. One of my friends and college mate Anandrao Mahadik let me stay in his office at Crawford Market. It was a 10x10 ft. room with a mattress to sit. There were no chairs and tables. His office time was 8 am to 7 pm. He had given me a key of his office. The agreement was that I would leave the office before 8 am and come after 7 pm and would make alternative arrangement in 10 days. My office time was from 9 am to 5 pm but no one left office before 6 pm. I would stay at my office till 7 pm and then after dinner in a restaurant, I would reach my abode by 9 pm. Within 10 days I found another place near Andheri railway station. It was a lodge-and-board arrangement with four people to a room. Everyone would keep his bag below his bed. There was common facility of toilet and bath. It was on first floor of a building. In my room were working people in the age group of 25 to 30. We all became friends.

I had paid advance rent and for dinner up to 31st December. I would eat lunch in a restaurant near the factory. I remember that on 25th of December I had exhausted my money. There was no money for afternoon meals and bus fare from Worli to Mahalaxmi station. I walked for 6 days. I ate roasted grams and nuts for 6 days. I could not ask for advance against my salary, as I had not completed even a month. I received the first salary of Rs 300 on 1st Jan 1965.

First lesson I learnt

I realized the importance of savings. I had earned quite a good amount during last two and half year of my service before termination but I did not save, therefore could get only one meal. I decided that I would save 30% of my take home pay from now onwards. I opened a recurring account and started saving. Later when I was in Dushkeda working as General Manager of a paper mill I wrote a small article about the importance of saving and distributed to all the young trainee engineers. They followed it and some of them write to me now that it has helped them in their financial stability. I give here under the text of my article for the young readers of this story.

"It is very necessary to cultivate the habit of saving money. This not only strengthens the financial position of an individual but also gives financial security, which is very necessary to avoid fear of unemployment. It is a practice, which requires day-to-day exercise. If an individual is able to make it his hobby, saving becomes easier. Everything has its cost. Saving too costs us something. The cost of saving is sacrifice. One has to sacrifice his pleasures, comforts, and even few necessities. Every individual has some habits like smoking, casual drinks, more often entertainment which does not contribute much utility, visiting the relatives and spending on un-necessary traveling during leave and so many others. If these habits are abandoned a sizeable amount can be saved.

Saving is most necessary in the young age though the income during this period is very less. In this age a man is strong and he can cultivate the habit of sacrifice and even pull on by cutting the necessities, but in the old age his body becomes weak, he requires more vitamins, nutrition, medical aid and at that time saving is not possible. If 30% of take home salary is saved every month after 10 years return of monthly interest of saving will be equivalent to the amount of salary. At the time of retirement he will be financially so strong that he will not feel the shortage of money in absence of social security schemes in India. Calculate for yourself and find out the truth and only then follow this advice".

This article was liked by District small saving department so much that while canvassing for small savings they gave example of this article.

Here it was my first experience in a manufacturing company. It was easy to teach Economics, Business Methods and Accountancy in a school but quite difficult to practice it in an industry. But soon I learned. I have always maintained that I am a lucky person. God always helped me whenever I needed help. When my services as a teacher were terminated I was sad and blamed God but he had something better in store for me.

Mr. Motisingh Chauhan

Mr. Motisingh Chauhan was the Manager of this manufacturing unit. We used to manufacture printed containers for Oil companies like Burmah shell, Caltex, Esso and other oil, chemical and pharmaceutical companies. The main raw material was Tin Plates which was a controlled item. It was the time of quota and permit regime. Permits were issued from Delhi and the management had a very good liaison officer at Delhi who managed this work. Mr. Chauhan was a very hardworking, sincere and disciplined person. Our office time was from 9.30 am to 5.30 pm. Mr. Chauhan would always come at 9.15 and never left the office before 6 pm. He was an old and trusted employee of Somanis and had come to this position, from a very lower level, because of his sincerity and honesty.

Mr. Devdutta Moondhra was an Accountant but he was more interested in local stores material purchases. After lunch he would always leave the office for market. Therefore there was a vacuum in Accounts Department.

My training started directly in the supervision of Mr Chauhan. Mr. Moondhra too helped and guided me. In one year I was able to draw final accounts. The Manager also gave me exposure of stores and finally raw material department. Our cost of raw material was more than 70 percent of the total cost. I was also given the work of raw material reconciliation with finished product, which was very important job in industry. If one knows the trick one can inflate or deflate profits.

BACHELOR LIFE IN BOMBAY

In the year 1965 I had ample time at my disposal on Saturday and Sunday. Almost every Sunday I went to Cooperage ground to witness football matches.

One day Anandrao called me. There was a program by the cultural ministry of Maharashtra. It was about the culture of Goa and Maharashtra. His uncle was the cultural Minister of Maharashtra. Anandrao had two passes in the 2nd row. He took me with him. In this program Lata Mangeshkar, Mukesh and Mohammed Rafi performed live. It was conducted by Ameen Sayani of Binaca Geetmala fame. Many actors and actresses also attended this program.

I also attended a kavisammelan in Rangbhavan presided over by Dev Anad the legendary actor. In this Kavisammelan poet Gopaldas "Neeraj", Indeevar, Shailendra and Anand Bakshi were also present. I think Neeraj came in contact with Dev Anand in this Kavisammelan. Later he wrote songs for Dev Anand's film 'Prem Pujari'.

I had also seen many films in cinema house like Maratha Mandir where film Mughale Azam was screened continuously for six years, Apsara theatre and Strand etc.

I was fond of eating outside in restaurants and dhabas on every Sunday. I visited famous restaurant Khaiber, Purohit, where food was served in silver ware and dhabas like Marwari dhaba near cotton exchange in Kalbadevi area, Thakkar club, Quality restaurant and Copper chimney.

OUR PICNIC TO TRIMBAKESHWAR A JYOTIRLINGA TEMPLE

During this period Mr. Moondhra arranged a picnic to Trimbakeshwar temple at Nasik for the residents of his building in which he was staying at Chembur. He also included the names of people like me who were working under him in the list. As I was from the city of Mahankaleshwar one of the jyotirlinga, I became anxious to visit Nasik. I did not know at that time that I was destined to make permanent abode in this city.

MY READING IN BOMBAY

In Bombay I faced some difficulty. I was from Hindi heart land therefore I not fluent in speaking and writing English. I felt that unless I improve my writing and speaking abilities in English it would be difficult to progress. I therefore started reading English short stories and novels. I read Pearl.S.Buck, Charles Dickens, D.H.Lawrence, Jeffrey Archer, Alexender Duma, Tolstoy, Alistair Stuart, MacLean, Ian Fleming, Oliver Strange, Sir Arthur Conan Doyle, Enid Blyton and many others. This helped a lot and removed the inferiority complex I had felt.

My promotion and marriage with Sumitra

In the beginning of the year 1966 I was promoted as Assistant Accountant. In the same year my mother fell ill. In spite of the best treatment available at that time she did not recover. She wished that I should be married. My father sent me the photo of a girl. Her name was Sumitra. My father wanted me to go to see her. I thought I recognized the photo. I have already written earlier about this girl. I thought she is the same girl.

Her father was an additional Civil surgeon at Sahdol, a district of Madhya Pradesh. I agreed and told my father that it was not necessary for me to see her. I was having my own views about marriage. If a man is honest, full of love and affection for his spouse and ready to support her in good and bad days he can lead happy life with any girl.

One of her relative Mr. Rudradutta Gupta called me at his residence at Tardeo in Mumbai and inquired about my work and me. Ananadrao Mahadik accompanied me. I was honest in telling him that I was Assistant Accountant and not the Accounts Officer. My salary was only Rs. 600 and lived in a guesthouse. He was quite an aged and Gandhian person. He liked my honesty and approved me. The marriage took place on 6th of May 1966. Within a week my mother died.

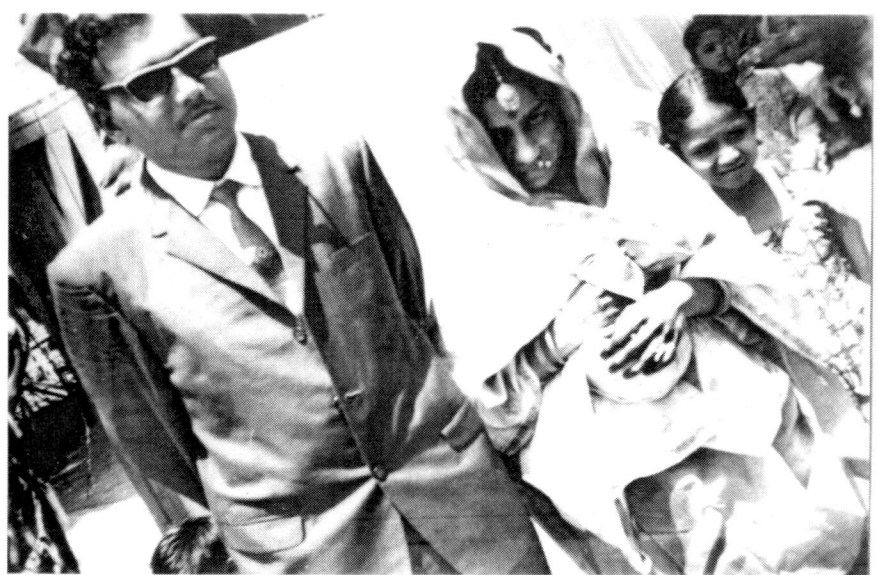

Marriage with Sumitra

SUMITRA'S ARRIVAL IN MUMBAI

I came back to Mumbai and rented a house in Dombivali, a suburb of Mumbai. After three or four months I brought her to Dombivali. It so happened that on that day Rickshaws had gone on strike. So we walked to our locality called Gopalnagar and the name of building was Sunmitra Sadan. It was one and half kilometer from railway station. Both of us had one attaché each. Hers was a little heavy and mine was light. We exchanged attaches. She walked behind me. I remembered the scene from the Nobel prize winning novel 'The Good Earth' written by Pearl S. Buck. Wang Lung brings his wife O Lane from the city to his village walking all the way. His wife walks behind him with her belongings on her head. They come to their thatched house. His wife immediately starts cooking for the family and friends. He becomes satisfied seeing that his wife was quite strong and will cultivate his fields with him. When we reached our one room kitchen house she did not say a word about her fatigue. I was happy to notice that she was quite strong and would walk easily with me on the uneven track of my life.

On reaching my shabby apartment she immediately took bath and started cooking. I had only one stove and few utensils. I had earlier purchased some spices, flour and Dal. While she cooked I took bath and then unpacked our clothes and kept in an open Almirah, which was provided in one of the walls of the room. She called me for our first dinner and gave me Khichadi. I was alarmed and became somewhat doubtful whether she knew cooking. But later she proved to be a very good cook.

I left for office at 7 am and returned by 9 pm. I was worried about how she will pass her time as she had never moved out of her state and did not know the Marathi language. But soon my fears were quelled.

She became very friendly with the girls of her age residing in that building. She started going to market with them. She acquired working knowledge of Marathi within a month and started speaking without any hesitation with them in six months time. She would bring ration from ration shop standing in queue. Now passing time was not a problem. She was good at stitching. She taught those girls how to stitch and mend clothes. Their parents were happy to notice seeing their girls sitting with her and learning.

BIRTH OF MY FIRST SON SUNDEEP

In November 11, 1967 my first son Sundeep was born at Sagar a district place in M.P where his Nanaji was working as Additional Civil Surgeon.

My health problem

It was my habit to reach office at 9 am and work till the manager left the office. There was no problem earlier when I was living near office in guesthouse. My office was at Worli Naka. However from Dombivali to reach my office I would start at 7 am and returned home by 9 pm. I would travel all the way standing in overcrowded local trains. Usually I walked from Worli to Mahalaxmi station in evening to catch the train. The distance was about 3 Km.

I started keeping unwell. My health was so good that no one could diagnose the disease. I attended office regularly. One day in May 1968 when I returned from office I ran a fever and coughed blood. Next day I went to see Dr Nene a chest specialist at Charni Raod Mumbai.

He diagnosed it as Lungs T.B and that too at a quite advanced stage having a cavity. When I asked the reason Doctor replied that this might be due to your overexertion and travelling in local train. Ten percent of the population is suffering from this disease due to overcrowded local trains in which one always inhales others breath. I had fallen victim to a contagious disease.

GOD AGAIN HELPED ME

Shri Rudradutta Gupta known as Dada again came to help me. He shifted me from Dombivali to Nanachowk in a flat of one of his acquaintance and sent me to Sagar (a district place of M.P) where my father-in—law was posted at that time. I was kept in a special ward of the civil hospital and recovered in 45 day, but I lost my good physique, gained weight due to rich diet given to me during this period. I was overweight now. I had to keep my son away for about six months. It was in his interest. My wife suffered and I saw her shedding tears silently in the middle of night many a times. I also missed the company of my only son who was eight months old at that time. Those were testing times during that period. One of my nearest relations commented many a times on how a mother could leave her eight months old son away. Every time such a comment was made she felt as if someone has hammered her heart. She could not explain to them that we were going through difficult times and it was the question of life and death for him. We kept him away in the interest of his health.

I joined my duties. Neither any one of my colleagues asked me about my disease nor did I say. Now it was quite easy to travel from Nanachowk to Worli. It was only 40 minutes journey. I got rid of disease in one year and was declared fully recovered. Our son Sundeep also joined us.

I am thankful to my colleagues P.R.Kabra, A.C.Joshi, K.C.Joshi, B.K.Toshniwal, A.C.Gour, Prabhakar, V.R.Menon and many others who gave me moral support during my bad days. They were all young persons who had started their career in this company. We were working like a family. Mr Motising Chauhan had built a good team of employees and trained them. I have no hesitation in accepting that he was a good administrator and trainer. He helped us in our progress and never harmed us.

I received excellent training in this firm. There was a change of partnership, dissolution of firm then conversion into a private limited company and finally a limited company. Our Auditors were Batliboi and Purohit. They had written and published their famous book "Accountancy by Batliboi and Purohit". It was prescribed as a textbook in my B.com course. One of the senior most partners at that time was a parsi gentlemen called Mr Berdi. He told me that I was lucky to witness so many changes that gave me an opportunity to handle different type of accounts. He said that there are many C.As' who never get to handle in their life time the dissolution accounts or conversion of partnership firm into a limited company. In nutshell I would like to say that my training was meaningful.

INFLUENCE OF SHRI HARISHANKAR DWIVEDI TAUJI ON MY LIFE

When dada shifted me to Nanachowk, I came in contact with Shri Harishankarji. I always addressed him as Tauji. He was a man of vast experience of life. He was an Ex-MLA and was Vice Chairman of All India Farmer Federation under the chairmanship of Prof. N.G. Ranga. He was in the working committee of League for Independence of India fathered by Pt. Nehru and Netaji Subhash Bose. He was the president of Adarsh Seva Sangh and Editor of Rural India, a journal dedicated to rural upliftment. He also stayed in that flat. He was very fond of milk. He used to take me often after dinner to take a glass of milk at the sweet meat shop at Grant Road. He was a very seasoned social worker. I never saw him angry. He would always encourage me to work with dedication. Many a times he said that object is never small or big. To achieve any object you need the same amount of dedication. Whenever we sat together he gave lectures to me on many subjects. He molded my outlook towards life. His routine started at 4 am and he worked till 11 pm.

Here I became one of his family members. His elder son Krantikumar, much elder to me, was an advocate in Gwalior and a jolly good fellow. Whenever he came to Mumbai we would go out for dinner. Bhabhi Sarla also treated me and my wife very well. His second son Ashok was a professor of military science in a college in Madhya Pradesh also became friendly with me. His wife Saroj was a lecturer in a college. Both treated us very well during our stay with them in Mumbai. I am proud of becoming a member of their family.

He is a well read person. He wrote commentary on Gita as "Essence of the Bhagwat Gita". He gave many discourses on Gita in USA. Tauji is 105 years of age now and staying in Gwalior.

PROMOTION AS ACCOUNTANT

Mr. D.D Mundra started his own business and resigned the job. I was promoted as an Accountant some time in 1967. It was my practice to sit in office up to 5 pm and clear the pending work on every Saturday though the office time was up to 2.30 pm. One Saturday when I was sitting in office our chairman Shri S.K. Somani wanted some details. He telephoned and asked if I can provide him those details. At that time he did not know me nor I had met him. I took the details to his office at Shrinwas house. He was very pleased. This was my first experience with him. He had a pleasing personality. He was a talkative person always smiling and aristocratic. I enjoyed his confidence. Later he helped me at many times in my promotions.

I was happy with my job. Sundeep our son had also came back to us. Darkness of night had ended and we saw the happy morning lights in our life.

MUNNI DAUGHTER OF SHRI RUDRADUTTA GUPTA (DADA)

Dada was staying at Taradeao, very near Nanachowk, a walking distance from my residence. His daughter Savitri known as Munni was a student. She became very attached to Sundeep. Every day after school hours she would come to our house and play with Sundeep. He too became restless if she did not come at her fixed time. He would be very delighted as soon as she came and would go straight to her. She would take him down to market where he liked to watch traffic. Sometimes she would take him to her house. She would help my wife with her daily shopping. She was born and brought up in Bombay and was fearless whereas my wife was afraid to cross streets and go alone in to shop. She was a great help to my family. Her two brothers Ramesh and Hari who were also school going children used to come to our place. Thus my wife never felt lonely.

Shri V.N. Khanna

While I was working in Oriental Containers apart from Motising Chauhan I was much impressed by Shri V.N.Khanna who was working as Sales Manager. He was a simple and soft-spoken person. He was a quiet person concerned with his work, having complete commitment to his duties. He constantly thought about his product satisfaction. If untimely rains occurred, even late in night, he would be the first person to reach the factory and ensure that all the finished products were safe in a shed. As far as I know he had never taken leave or attended any function out of Bombay. Once or twice he might have gone out of Bombay but on return came directly from Airport to factory. I found many similarities in Mr. Bidani and him. When I closely watched Sarvshree Bidani, Motisingh Chauhan and V.N. Khanna it gave strength to my conviction that there is no substitute to hard work. I, therefore, started following their footsteps.

Transfer to Calcutta

Now life had become easy for me but God had decided again to test my energy. In the end of 1969 I was transferred to Calcutta as a Secretary of a company. There was a company known as Shri Engineering Products Ltd making malleable steel products for Automobile and other Industries but mainly for Hindustan Motors and Jaishree Insulators Ltd. Shri Narayandas Mimani who was the younger brother of Shri Bhairavdas Mimani managed the unit. The later one was the brother-in-law (sister's husband) of Shri K.K. Somani. Both were highly educated persons. Mr. Mimani was an engineer and had taken training in Germany. Mr. Somani was B.E. Electrical and Mechanical. Here first time I came in contact with Shri K.K. Somani popularly known as K.K. Babu, who from his Bombay office visited the factory at Calcutta once in a month. I saw in him a real industrialist, who was ready to sacrifice everything for the sake of industry. He was quite a simple man practicing austerity in his daily life. At that time little did I know that I would have the longest association with him for almost 30 years. I learned many lessons from him during my association with him.

How I gained knowledge of labour Laws

I was well trained in commercial activities but had no knowledge of labour matters. I think God wanted me to take training of Labour matters for my future promotion. At that time Naxalite movement was on its peak in west Bengal. Everyone was afraid to work in Calcutta on a responsible position. I was in Rishra an Industrial suburb of Calcutta. Workers used to sleep in the night shift therefore there was loss of production. Some workers would threaten the timekeepers and get their attendance marked and leave the factory. Supervisors were afraid. The factory was running at a loss. I reported this matter to K.K Babu who wanted discipline in factory. He instructed me to take disciplinary action against errant workers. I suspended seven workers. As a result there was some violence. I was advised to declare lockout.

During the period of lockout, one person who was very senior in handling labour matters was the Manager human resources in Shri Digvijay Cement Company, known as Panditji was sent to Calcutta to assess the gravity of situation. He was known to K.K. Babu, who was had been the Managing Director of Shri Digvijay Cement Company once. Panditji was a very mature person. He listened to me very patiently. Thereafter he visited Calcutta several times and gave many lectures to me on labour problems and how to handle them. In a nutshell he told me that labour has become undisciplined due to Government policies. There are many restrictions on employers but no check on labour. Therefore one has to deal with patience. It is an art and differs from manager to manager. However things were not improving. He advised the management to declare closure. I issued the notice of closure as occupier. He advised me to read all the Acts applicable to factory such as Factories Act, Industrial Dispute Act, Payment of wages Act, Bonus Act and so on. I read all these Acts. I was already knowledgeable of the bonus Act. I had several times calculated bonus as per act but there was one overriding provision, which killed the very spirit of Act that was the unions were given freedom to negotiate for the higher amount of bonus. This provision made the whole Act redundant. Workers never agreed to the calculation. One of their prominent labour leaders of Bombay Dr. Dutta Samant openly declared that all the Accounts of companies are manipulated and he outright rejected the very basis of calculation.

I again had to keep my family away. My wife and Sundeep had to stay with my elder brother at Delhi for six months. I faced strike, lockout and closure of factory within a very short period of time. It was an excruciating experience for me.

A THREATENING LETTER

During the closure period I received a threatening letter by post as under:

"MOU SETUN LAL SELAM WARNING

To K. G. Gupta

You are a capitalist and cheat the workers of the factory. You hate Bengalis. If you do not leave Bengal with in a month you will be murdered. Be careful Satan."

I have still kept that letter with me. Whenever I received such threatening letters in future I read this and get strength to fight. The Manager of Kaimerbagshaw Ltd and Kusum products Ltd received a similar letter. They proceeded on a long leave but I stayed. I consider it my biggest folly now. But it was a blessing in disguise. It improved my image with factory workers. After some time union leader Shri Jodugopal Sen worked out a solution. Everything ended well. The Factory started functioning. My wife and son came back to Calcutta to live with me.

SUNDEEP FRACTURED HIS LEG

Here on one evening at about 4 pm when it was raining heavily, Sundeep was watching the rain from a window of first floor of my house, which was inside the factory. He fell down from the window. God saved him as he fell just a foot away from the Brick divider. There was a fracture in his knee. It was raining heavily on that day. I could not take him to the doctor. The boy showed great strength. Must have been in pain the whole night but he never complained. Next day though it was still raining I took him on a cycle rickshaw to an orthopedic doctor who plastered his leg. For three months he was in a bed. God helped me again. Had he fallen on his head first it would have been a great tragedy.

In 1971 Bangladesh war took place. The excitement all over Calcutta was worth watching. The Victory was celebrated with great fanfare.

BACK TO BOMBAY

In the later part of 1971 a person who was working as a Company Secretary in Oriental container at Bombay resigned. I was called back to Bombay. Shri Dwivediji was kind enough to accommodate me again in his flat at Nanachowk.

On 28th Feb 1972 my second son Amit was born. I was a strong supporter of family planning. I underwent vasectomy operation on the same day in Bombay Hospital.

During this time Company secretary's rules came in force. Every company having a capital of 25 lacs should have a qualified secretary. Those who were already working as secretary were allowed to register with the Institute of company Secretaries in order to obtain a certificate without passing any examination. I decided to acquire qualification and registered myself for the course. I passed Intermediate exam in 1973 without any difficulty.

RAJENDRA SOMANI

If I remember correctly Shri Rajendra Somani had started looking after the affairs of Oriental Containers Limited In the year 1972. He was the son of Shri S.K.Somani who had a soft corner for me and suggested my name whenever an experienced young person was required in some other factory. Oriental was a sort of training institution for me. I did not come in his contact for a long time. However he was a young man. I observed that he was always smiling and, whenever laughed he laughed heartily. I found him sensitive and ready to help his employees in time of their need. Even at such a young age he had a sharp sense of business. He could navigate the business of Oriental successfully during the testing times.

Even when the business was at its low he did not resort to retrenchment of employees. People who were working along with me in the Oriental in those days are still with him though they have crossed the age of seventy years. When I informed him about my project of a movable morgue in the year 2009 he was the person who appreciated it very much. In fact it was he who suggested that the name should be given as "Antim Chaya" instead of movable morgue. He recently published a collection of his poems under the name of 'Nirmal Anand' which is an evidence of his emotional and poetic heart. I felt honored when he remembered me and sent me a copy of his book.

TRANSFERRED TO NASIK

In early 1974 I was transferred to Nasik as Factory Manager of Citric India and Shri Vindhya paper mills Ltd. I had to take charge from Shri T.T. Dulani, who was manager and due for retirement. I rented a bungalow here having 3 rooms, kitchen and a small garden. After staying in Bombay in a small apartment of one Room and Kitchen it was a dream come true for me. We were all happy to have such a big house. St Philomena an English medium school was behind our house. Sundeep was admitted there. He was a very intelligent and studious boy. He was liked by all the teachers so when I tried for admission of my younger son I did not face any difficulty.

Life again was easy here. In lunch time we would get a Tiffin from our house and enjoyed our lunch together. All of the senior employees were living like a family.

SHRI. SUSHEEL SOMANI

Both the factories were under the same management. K. K. Babu was looking after technical aspect of both the factories as well as complete working of Shri Vindya paper mills. His younger brother Susheel Somani was taking care of the process and production of Cirtic India Ltd. He had a M.Sc. degree in science and was well experienced person. I had no difficulty with the management as I had worked with K. K. Babu earlier and Susheel Somani was a real gentleman, a very well behaved person. He never allowed us to feel that we were employees and that he was the owner. He used to enjoy beer in the evening and invited us many times for dinner in Guesthouse where he stayed. He had two sons of the same age as of my sons. Whenever they visited Nasik Mrs. Kumkum Somani his wife will always invite my sons to play with them.

God called me for Darshan

Our company owned a guesthouse known as Windy Hall. It was in the cantonment area of Devlali, a very beautiful locality. There were 6 or 8 rooms, dining hall and a kitchen a big garden and a tennis court. Whenever Susheel Somani visited we had a party. In fact we always waited for his visit. In 1975 Mr. Dulani and I were sitting in the hall of the guesthouse. I asked Dulaniji if he had visited Tirupati Balaji. Mr. Dulani replied affirmatively. I said I wish I could visit the temple. After some time Mr. Susheel Somani came down from his room. We had dinner together. When we were just ready to depart he asked me if I would like to visit Tirupati. I was dumb founded. He had booked two plane tickets to Bangalore for the next day evening but the other person expressed his inability to join him due to some urgent work. Next day by morning train I reached Bombay at 11 am and joined him at the airport to catch 2.30 pm flight. We reached Banglore and stayed in a guesthouse of West Coast Paper Mills overnight. Next day by car we departed for Tirupati Balaji Temple, about 225 km from Bangalore. We had Darshan in the evening. Next day was Friday. We performed Abhishekam puja in the morning. Only 100 persons were allowed at that time in that puja. He had made all the arrangements in advance. We returned next day by car to Bangalore and by air to Bombay on the same day. I returned to Nasik by 11 pm on the same day. I had never imagined even in my dream that I would have such a wonderful darshan.

AGAIN I HAD DARSHAN

Next year when I was on a visit to Bombay office at about 12 noon he suddenly came to me and asked if I would like to come with him to Tirupati as one of his friends Mr. Porecha, who was a share broker, for whom plane ticket was reserved could not make it. I told him that I have no clothes, as I had not planned for a night stay in Bombay. He advised me to purchase some readymade clothes from a store. He arranged for payment through his cashier. I again had the Abhisekam puja in the same Royal way travelling by Air and car and staying in Padmawati guesthouse. Mr. Susheel Somani was a very kind hearted person and I am thankful to him for my first Darshan of Tirupati, which otherwise I would never have dreamt. He is such a nice person that even when I left services whenever he came to Nasik he met me and once or twice he stayed with me.

Since then it so happened that I visited Tirupati Balaji Temple every year with my family up to 2008. Once in the year 1984 chairman Shri S.K.Somani decided to perform all the seven days puja at Tirupati temple. He called me to accompany him. I joined him and had all the pujas performed with his family. Once I had also visited Tirupati temple with K.K Babu and his family. After 2008 it became very difficult for me to reach there and perform such pujas.

MY JOB AND COLLEAGUES

Shri Dulaniji retired sometimes early in the year 1975. I took full charge of administration. Though I had passed intermediate exam of company Secretary course in 1973 I could not appear for final exam in 1974 due to my new job. In 1975 I completed my Company Secretary course and obtained a certificate from the Institute of Company Secretaries.

Now I was well settled in my job. I improved public relations. Established excellent relation with executives of other industrial units and Nasik Industrial Manufacturer Association's members popularly known as NIMA. I also maintained good relations with Government Authorities. This resulted in obtaining some sizable and profitable supply orders of paper from these departments. When my performance appraisal was done I think it was to the satisfaction of Management.

Here I would like to add few lines about my colleagues.

Shri J.N Maheshwari was the stores officer of Citric India. He was very systematic. Stores were kept very tidy. He was so particular that he would not tolerate a little mistake on the part of his assistant. I am sure his wife must have faced many difficulties in the up keep of house to his satisfaction.

Shri S.G. Jhavar was the stores officer of Shri Vindhya paper mills Ltd. He was very accomodating and a well-behaved person.

Mr. Butch, works Manager of Citric India Ltd was a Gujarati gentleman. He was always ready to help people. I many a times jokingly said to him that "Butch sahib, you will not hesitate to help a man to find a dagger even if he wanted to stab you."

Mr. D.D.Biyani, works manager of Shri Vindhya paper mills was another character who was always cutting jokes. He could never be serious. Even when he was annoyed and wanted to scold his subordinates he would not be able to remain serious and turn him out laughingly. He was a chronic patient of Asthma. I had many times seen attack of asthma on him and wondered how this man is so humorous.

Shri D.D.Sharma, who was production manager and was promoted to the position of General Manager when D.D.Biyani left. He was a simple man, always tied to his work and was a thorough gentleman but by nature a reserved person.

Mr. H.S.Makwana was an outstanding person having engineering skills. He was a born engineer. There was no mechanical engineering problem that he could not have solved. I would like to write in details about him later.

Chief Engineer, Goel Saheb, was quite an aged and respected person having a fatherly attitude towards all of us.

I would like to mention the names of four persons whom I found extraordinarily sincere and diligent. I had appointed them in commercial department of both the companies. A.S.Vispute, V.M.Deshmukh and Asim Chakraborty. I trained them directly under my supervision. Later I heard that they resigned and joined some other companies. However they proved their talent and retired as the senior executives.

Fourth one was Shri Hanumansingh Gahlot who was referred to me by Shri Motisingh Chauhan, under whom I had taken training in Oriental containers Ltd. I trained him in various departments of the mill. Later he proved to be a great help to me.

MRS AND MR SUNDER, THEIR SON NIKETH AND THEIR DAUGHTER NEENA

Adjacent to my bungalow there was another bungalow in which Mrs. and Mr. Sunder lived with their son and a daughter. Mr. Sunder was an officer in Hindustan Aeronautic Ltd. where our MIG Fighters are produced. Mrs. Sunder was a teacher in St. Philomena Convent School. My son Sundeep was admitted in this school. He became very friendly with Niki and Neena though he was much younger to them. They have played very important role in his development. I was always busy in my work. Sundeep's mother, though a graduate was not able to speak English. This family was always conversing in English at their home. Sundeep started passing his time in their house with these two children. Niki and Neena guided him in completing his homework. His strong base was made because of these two children. Mrs Sunder also took much pain to improve his understanding. She took him on tours organized by the school. He visited Kashmir, Nepal and Shri Lanka with her. Because of the help of this family Sundeep could later secure seventh position in the Merit list of Pune Board for Higher Secondary Examination. Niki joined Indian Navy and after completing his training from NDA Khadakwasala and after few years of service he became a

Commodore. Neena known as Anushka Ravi Shankar is a well-known writer of many books. As a mark of my respect to this family I feel it necessary to write a few lines about them.

MR. SHRIRAM DAMLE AND HIS DAUGHTER SARITA

I was a member of India Security Press Gymkhana at Nasik Road. I had joined the Gymkhana to play Badminton, table tennis and Billiards. One day I met Shriram Damle. He had also come to play Badminton. On that day there were only four players present so he became my partner. We played many games. He had a jolly good nature. Next day when I asked about his work he informed that he was transferred from Nagpur as the superintending Engineer of MSEB. He had three daughters. His family was likely to join him after three months when the exams of his daughters are over. We became good friends. As he was alone he came to play every day. After the games we used to go to our guesthouse or to my residence for dinner. Often we would sit at his residence. He had a good cook who made different type of dishes. Later when his family came to Nasik they regularly visited my house. His elder daughter Sarita was very jovial. She became friend of both my sons. Later when Shri Damle was transferred from Nasik to Bombay as the Secretary of the Board his Daughter Sarita remained in Nasik. She stayed a few days with me and later took admission for MBA and moved to the hostel of her college in Nasik. My name was given as the Local Guardian. She would visit my children every Sunday at our residence or I would see her in her hostel in my green colour Ambassador car carrying hot breakfast for her. The car became famous as a matter of joke in hostel compound because of its peculiar color. Few of her roommates were always asking her when the green car will come. I am sure she was sharing breakfast with them. Later she was married and is settled in Pune. When my younger son Amit took admission in one of the Engineering college of Pune known as MIT she became his local guardian and took care of him. She still treats both my sons as her brothers and never forgets to send them Rakhi.

LAKSH CHANDI YAGNA WAS PERFORMED

In the year 1976 management of Citric India decided to initiate a Laksh chandi yagna. In this yagna one hundred thousand AHUTIS were to be given with the mantras. It was a program of seven days. All the family members of Somanis came to perform it. I was given the responsibility of chief Yajman. I sat in the Yagna with my wife for seven days. Again on the last day at Purnahuti all the members of the family came. I am thankful to God who provided me an opportunity to serve such pious people having unstinted faith in religion and got a chance to perform this puja which otherwise I would never had performed.

VISIT OF THE DADA
(PANDURANGJI SHASHTRI
AHAVALE)

In the year 1977 Pandurangji Shastri Athavale known as Dada visited our factory. He stayed in our guesthouse. He was one of the great saints. He was a reformer. He worked in Maharashtra and Gujrat for the upliftment of down trodden people in remote areas of these two states. K.K Babu also accompanied him. I felt lucky to sit in his company along with other dignitaries.

K. G. Gupta garlanding Dada

Great event and a test of my organizational skill

In the year 1978 a great event was organized in Nasik Road. It was given the name of 'Rashtriya Navratri Utsav'. As all the prominent citizens of Nasik Road knew my public relation work I was therefore elected as the Chairman. Appasaheb Aringle who was the president of Nasik Road Municipality was patron-in-chief.Patron in Chief

Our Chief guests included Shri V.V.Shirwadkar, popularly known as Kusumagraj, who was a well known literary figure and recipient of Sahitya academy award and Gyanpeeth Puruskar, and Shri Dada Saheb Potnis owner and editor of 'Gavkari' a widely circulated news paper in Maharashra. It was organized on a grand scale. It was eight days program. People remembered it for many years.

A big pandal was erected on India Security press ground capable of accommodating about 10000 people.

The program was as under.

3rd October 1978 Bismillakhan and party (Sahanai)

4th October 1978 Musical Night by Shri Jaywant Kulkarni and Pushpa Pagadhare and party.

5th   October 1978 Melody Night Talat Mahmood and Minoo Purushottam.

6th   October 1978 Loknatya: "Gadhvache Lagna" by Vag Samarat Dadu Indulkaar and Mahu Kadu.

7th   October 1978 Variety entertainment by Sound and Symphony Orchestra.

8th   October 1978 Folk Dances of India Nite by Gopi krishna and Party.

9th   October 1978 Ramleela by Gadhwal Sanskritik Mandal Bombay.

10th October 1978 Qawalli night by Ysuf Azad and Mahalka Banu.

Bismillakhan Saheb

We wanted to make our program a great success; therefore we began with Bismillakhan Sahib on the very first day. He had already acquired fame from "Gunj Uthi Shehnai" film. We had kept purposely his program on first day considering that the first impression is last impression. The program was a grand success. I have no words to express. The program opened at 9 pm and continued till 1 am. No one got up even to attend the call of nature. Everyone was engrossed in listening to his Shehnai. He finished with the song of film "Gunj uthi Shehnai". I had made arrangements of his stay in a Christian Sanatorium near our program venue. He had arrived by morning train. I asked him if he wanted anything special. He demanded Halua (Seera). He asked me if I know how to prepare. I declined. He then told me "Hamri bahu ko ley awo ham samjha denge." I brought my wife with me. His recipe for Halua was as as under.

One katori Ata, Two Katori Ghee, Three katori Sugar, Four Katori water.

He explained that for Shehnai wadak Ghee and sugar is necessary tonic for throat. He was a very simple man. At that time photographs were not so common. Unfortunately I have no photograph of him with me.

TALAT MAHMOOD

On 5th of October a crowd of near 12,000 people came to hear Talat Mahmood. We purposely had not invited any chief guest for that day. The program started without any formality, as it was difficult to control the crowd.

On 6th October there was a natya (drama) called "Gadvache Lagna'. Many people from nearby villages started pouring in by bullock carts and buses. They continued to arrive the whole day. By evening the crowd swelled to 20,000. Appasaheb Aringle was the chief guest on that day. I called him at about 6 pm and requested him to visit the ground. He came and on seeing the crowd he immediately telephoned the collector and D.S.P. They arranged a company of SRP to maintain law and order. In those days Dadu was quite famous and his Natya 'Gadvache Lagna' was a roaring success in all the parts of Maharashtra.

FIRE BY SHORT CIRCUIT AND DANCE OF GOPIKRISHNA

On 8th of October at about 7 pm due to short circuit our stage caught fire and was completely destroyed. Gopikrishna had already arrived in hotel and was getting ready for his dance. He heard about the fire. He made it clear that he would not return without performing, even if he had to perform on plain ground. For him returning without performance was a bad omen. He was adamant.

I called the meeting of working committee. I have realized that God has given me extra strength to face such extremities. All the members were young. I would like to name few of them. Gangaprakash, Kamataprasad, later both of them held top positions in India Security Press, Malve and T.N.Adke Union leaders, O.P.Khanna, J.D.Kulkarni, D.K.Agrawal and many more.

Collector Mr. Basak and General Manager of India Security Press Mr. Mukherji came without any delay. We decided to make immediate alternate arrangements. Labour contractor Ismail Wahab of my Mill immediately arranged 100 laborers. Appasaheb arranged road rollers. The remains were cleared and ground was made smooth. Mr. Mukharji provided big tables from I.S.P and by 9 pm a temporary stage was ready.

No one could believe that this was a site of a serious calamity a few hours ago.

Gopikrishna started performing. He performed as if he was very angry. He himself performed continuously for 4 hours and only then his group joined in the dancing. After some time again Gopikrishna returned back on stage and started dancing as if some 'junun' has captivated him. It seemed as if he was in trance. He danced up to 3 am. It was a fantastic performance on his part. I had seen him in a film "Jhanak Jhanak Payal Baje". Here it was a live performance. People sat motionless. There was pin drop silence. We had never seen in our life such a spell binding performance. It was sheer enchanting show on his part. At 3 am in the morning he stopped as if something which was the cause of his anger has subsided inside him. He started smiling. Later he said he was very happy to perform on an open stage.

He further publicly stated that he had never got so much satisfaction from his performance in past. It was somewhat a unique experience for him too

YUUF AZAD AND MHELKA BANAU

, the 10th of October, was a program of Qawalli.
On the as smaller in comparison to earlier days. Only
The ng listeners were present. India security press
Hir he finance Ministry of Government of India. One
etary of Finance department and other persons
i had come to visit the press. They also attended
ram. Yusuf Azad was a well-known name in the field
valli at that time. He started his program at 9 pm and
at 1 am.

s the total program was a memorable event. It made
e quite popular in Nasik. My experience of extracurricular
activities of college days helped me in managing such a great
show successfully. Now my life was very easy. I had forgotten
the plight of earlier days.

While I was serving in Bombay, Somanis' constructed a colony
named as Mahesh nagar in Goregaon west. It was a cluster
of many buildings. Two or three buildings were combined to
make a Society. I was chairman of one of the society. Many
employees booked flats there. I too booked a flat of two
bedroom kitchen and measuring 550 sq feet. Total cost was Rs
12,000. Management granted us the entire amount as interest
free advance to be paid in installments. I could not stay in that

flat when possession was given I was al~dy transferred to
Nasik. I sold that flat for Rs. 80,000 in 197~d bought a flat
in Nasik. The Total area of the flat was 180 feet and the
cost was Rs. 98,000. I shifted to that house i~ 1979.

CONSTRUCTION OF TWO BUILDINGS FOR MEMBERS OF STAFF

Early in 1979 Shri V.M.Deshmukh, Vishpute and Chakraborty approached me. They were living in a rented house. Everyone has a dream that he should own his shelter. They also wanted their own house. They requested me to help them in this matter. They wanted an advance to book a flat in the buildings which were being constructed at Nasik Road. I suggested K.K. Babu to grant advance so that every member of staff might have his own flat. He agreed to grant interest free loans to be repaid in easy installments. But the idea did not work. The cost of flat was out of reach of the employees. These three boys calculated the cost of constructing a building of their own.

They short-listed a plot of land. As I have written earlier that I had seen in these boys future executives. I checked their calculation and found the idea workable. I advanced them Rs 60,000 for purchase of plot from my own funds which they refunded later. After taking possession of plot they registered a co-operative society as Dronagiri Co-operative housing society. K.K. Babu as promised granted loan to each one. Balance amount they raised as loan from Maharashtra Housing Finance Corporation. The construction started through the contractor on fixed labour rates. We supplied material. At that time cement was in short supply. It was commanding very high premium in market. K.K. Babu arranged the cement at controlled rates from Digvijay Cement company, where he had been Managing Director earlier. This way the first building was completed in early 1981 and possession of sixteen flats was given to the members at half of the market price.

When this trio started the construction of the first building other members of staff who were at that time doubtful about the success of project now believed in it. They too approached them for help. Again in 1980 I advanced them Rs70,000 for purchase of plot. They also refunded this amount on grant of loan by MHFC Ltd. The second society was registered as Gulshan Co-operative Housing society Ltd. With the help of K.K. Babu 14 flats were handed over to members in 1981 end. Thus I was instrumental in arranging for 30 members of staff their dream home.

PAPER PROJECT

I had earlier written that K.K. Babu was a real industrialist. His vision about industry was very clear. Many times he said profit or loss should not be the main objective of running an industry, but the main objective should be to run it efficiently and productivity should be kept in mind. He believed and practiced in simple living and high thinking. In the year 1978 he conceived a project of a paper mill.

The present mill was a processing unit. We were purchasing paper, our main raw material from other paper mills like Andhra Pradesh paper mills, West coast Papers and J.K. Papers etc. He thought of putting up his own paper mill. He started a survey for the best location. Many times I accompanied him. He finally finalized the location 10 km away from Bhusawal near Railway station Dushkheda on the bank of river Tapi. Main requirement of paper mill is water. Our site was down side from a Power house for which water was continuously released. Excess water was flowing down and we never felt shortage of water. I do remember that I was given responsibility to pay the amount to land holders. In the month of May the hottest days of the summer, I, along with Ratansi Vaid and his father Vallabh Seth who were supplying coal to our Nasik unit and stationed at Jalgaon about 40 km from our site, reached Dushkeda village with considerable amount of cash without any security personnel and made the payment. The Land was acquired and possession was given to us.

Shri Clay Products

In the mean time I read about a project of Brick Making from Fly Ash, the waste by-product from burning coal at the Power House. Its disposal was a problem for the Nasik Power House and they were giving it free of cost. I brought it to the notice of K.K. Babu who encouraged me. He helped me monetarily. I purchased the land and bought machinery. The project was started in record time and gained much publicity. General Manager of Industries department quoted everywhere in his lecture about how to manage and plan a project so that one can complete it in record time. I started this project in the name of Shri Clay Products. But I had to resign my present Job. I resigned in December 1980 and devoted full time to this project.

End of my life story from 1965 to 1980

PART THREE

MY LIFE STORY FROM 1981 TO 1990

SHRI CLAY PRODUCTS

I started the Brick factory in full swing from January 1981 and achieved the rated capacity. The bricks were tested in Maharashtra Engineering Research Institute (MERI). It passed all the specifications and physical properties. In those days construction activities were in full swing in Nasik therefore there was a good demand for bricks. I faced resistance from the masons. They started demanding money from me for the use of bricks. Many started rejecting on flimsy grounds. They would advise the builders of private houses saying that the wall may fall after few years. I knew that whenever a new product is launched such type of resistance was common. I showed them the testing results. Because of the shortage in market I could sell my entire production and by the year end June, which is normal for brick making, as rains start in June, the first year operation ended in some profit.

AGAIN I WAS CALLED BY K.K. BABU AND MY APPOINTMENT AS GENERAL MANAGER

K.K. Babu called me in the month of July. He asked me to join him again and look after Bhusawal plant. There was some vacuum and work was not progressing as per his schedule. It was a big project in size, largest in the district of Jalgaon. Those who had given land and were offered job had also become impatient. The progress was very slow. He offered me the position of General Manager and agreed not to appoint any one above me even after factory was operational. He also assured me that I would have total control of the factory. I asked some time to consider the proposal though he wanted me to proceed immediately. This is the first time I realized how much faith he had in me. He on his part kept all his promises given to me and fully supported me in all the decisions I had taken during my services under him.

It was a difficult decision for me to take. At this time my age was 41 years. My elder son was studying in 8th and younger one was in 4th standard. This factory was 10 km away from Bhusawal at village Dushkheda where there was no facility for education. Even in Bhusawal there was no proper facility for good education compared to Nasik. Moreover my elder son refused to shift to Dhuskeda. The younger one was very much attached to elder one so he also refused. My wife also suggested that I should not spoil their career. In short if I took the decision in favour I would have to go alone. It was not the matter of one or two years. It was for 5 years till my elder son completes his 12th standard and younger one at least 8th standard.

As mentioned earlier I enjoyed working with K.K. Babu. He was very honest in keeping his words and dedicated person to the development of industries. Taking quick decisions was one of his virtues. I decided to join him again. I discussed the matter in detail with my wife. She was very cooperative since beginning and had never argued against the decisions I had taken. She agreed to stay with my sons so that proper care is taken. I could imagine how much difficulty she might have faced to manage both the sons, without the supervision of their father, who were attaining the adolescence age. Entire credit goes to her that both the sons progressed well in their education.

I conveyed my acceptance. He issued the necessary orders and informed all the person concerned. Necessary power of attorney was given in my favour.

MY FIRST DAY AT FACTORY SITE

After settling all the pending matters at Nasik I reached Duskheda in mid August. They made my stay arrangements in a Government Guesthouse at Bhusawal. I reached the guesthouse in evening.

Mr. M.D. Khan a retired deputy collector was appointed as Liaison Officer of the company. He met me in the guesthouse and apprised me of the past progress and the present conditions at site. He came next morning and both of us boarded a train to reach the factory site. It was the next station from Bhusawal after crossing a bridge over river Tapi.

There were only two trains, once in morning and evening. The train started from Bhusawal at 9 am and we reached our site at Duskheda at 9.20. We walked from station to factory, as there was only muddy kachha village road in those days. The night before it had rained heavily so it was difficult to walk. Both of us took out our shoes and carried them in our hands. One more gentleman of my age also alighted the train and walked with us. All the three of us reached the site. This third gentleman Mr. Shyam Deshpande, later introduced himself as a practicing Chartered Accountant. He was inclined to take local audit of company. Later when M.D. asked me about my recommendation on many names he had received from Jalgaon I recommended the name of Shri

Shyam Deshpande, partner of Despande and Deshpande. While recommending his name I mainly considered his visit to factory as no other Chartered accountant had visited. He was the only person who wanted to see, what we were doing, before accepting the job.

I saw that the construction of factory building was in progress. Temporary roads had been constructed. Stores building were almost complete.

There were 12 rooms with common walls and roof of asbestos sheets constructed for staff working at site. There was no toilet facility, no drinking water and proper arrangement of kitchen and dining rooms. Rain was creating havoc and making life miserable. Staff was demoralized to its lowest level. There was no coordination. For every decision they had to depend on Bombay office. Though M.D. was prompt in taking decision but it took minimum 7 days time for a letter to reach Mumbai and back at site.

SHRI N. L. BHATIA

Here I would admire Mr. N. L. Bhatia who was an Electrical Engineer and coordinating the activities at Bombay Office. He was the same person who had taken charge from me in Calcutta when I was transferred from Shri Engineering products Ltd to Bombay. Later we worked together in Nasik too. He was a person of outstanding capabilities. I have no hesitation to admit here that without his support I would never have been successful at site in my work. Both of us fought on many issues but remained good friends working with one motto that was the progress of company.

H. S. MAKWANA

The second person that was at site was Mr. H.S.Makwana, commonly called as Kakaji. I have already written about him that he was a born engineer. He had kept all the staff members at site knit in a bond. He was the person who had returned from England after dismantling and dispatch of paper machine that was to be installed here. With him other supervisors and workers who had gone to England were also present and working. Their main work would start after the machine reached the site. The Civil Engineer was carrying out the main work.

Shri Hanuman Singh who had worked with me at Nasik was also present there. He was working as stores and purchase officer taking care of local requirements.

I devoted full time by walking around the site and discussing various matters of progress of work, their requirement and living conditions. I heard all of them patiently. By evening train Mr. Khan and I returned to the Guesthouse. When I was leaving I saw an expression on their face clearly. They were imploring me not to leave them. They wanted me to stay with them. Mr Khan was very matured person. He was honest in expressing his views. He told me frankly that the way the things are moving it will be difficult to complete the construction and few people had already left and others are waiting to leave.

I too was horrified looking at the conditions prevailing at site. Mr. Khan wanted to take me for dinner but I was not having any appetite after seeing those conditions and the enormous task I had to undertake. I realized that accepting the position of G.M. was easy but to fulfill the aspiration of management with limited resources will be a herculean task.

MY DILEMMA

I was worried. I was depressed and during this state of mind once I thought I should run away by the first available train the next morning and inform K.K. Babu about my inability to accept the job. Over the years I had developed a habit of introspection. Every day before going to bed I review my deeds of the day and try to learn from any mistakes. That day before going to bed I also performed my introspection routine. I considered my acceptance of the job and promise I made to K.K. Babu. I thought about his faith in me. During the process of introspection I also saw the faces of people working at the site as if imploring me to stay. I am a person of fighting spirit. For a short amount of time I get nervous but soon this spirit takes command of me. This spirit had helped me in Calcutta when I had received a threatening letter. The spirit had helped me when there was a fire in Rashtriya Navratri Utsav in Nasik.

The same spirit over powered me again after introspection. I took my decision and left everything to God. I slept a sound sleep. Next morning I telephoned to send me the jeep at the guesthouse. Mr. Khan also arrived in the morning. I packed my luggage. I told Mr. Khan that I would be staying at the site factory site at Dushkeda. He was dumb founded. Both of us started in the Jeep towards the site. After crossing the bridge over river Tapi, we took a right turn for the factory. I saw that there were no roads. It took us 40 minutes to cover the distance of 8 km from that turn. At last we reached the factory.

MY STAY AT THE SITE

I told all the people working at the site that I would be staying with them. I could immediately see a smile on their faces. They became cheerful. I decided to construct two toilet blocks, one kitchen and one dining room in the row of existing ten rooms. I occupied a vacant room. On that day after the end of the work, we discussed the future plans up to mid night. I was aware that work cannot go on without the free flow of booze and I therefore allowed few of them who enjoyed it. Labour contractor Ismail Wahab was always ready to help them. He was the same person who had worked with me in Nasik and erected the temporary stage after the fire in Navratri program in Nasik.

I do not know whether speed of work improved but I saw the faces which where ash brazen before now had a line of shine. Working conditions started improving. I had no specific work. Engineers were working at site. I started my temporary office in my room itself. I appointed a carpenter who from the packing wood made chairs and tables. I also got a dining table and few benches made for the dining room.

I made it a habit of taking lunch and dinner with the working persons. I made it my practice to see that they get breakfast at 8 am so that work can be started by 8.30 am. For lunch they were allowed to come whenever they got time. I made it my practice to see that everyone gets hot meals. I, as far a possible, tried to take lunch with the last batch. Mr. Khan was of great help to us. He was the eldest amongst us and treated us as his sons. While coming from Jalgoan he used to bring fresh vegetables and fruits. Work was gaining speed but sometimes due to heavy rains it had to stop.

I had promised my wife and children that I would visit them every 15 days but due to the love and affection of staff members and exigencies of work I could not fulfill my promise. My elder son Sundeep had always shown maturity more than his age therefore when my wife explained to him about my absence he understood my difficulties. Younger one was more attached to his mother and his elder brother so he never felt my absence.

Next month when I intended to go to Nasik I fell sick. The night before suddenly I caught high fever. The village doctor was called who gave me an injection. Next morning though the fever had come down but I felt burning sensation in my chest. I was taken to a Doctor at Bhusawal who gave me a injection of Vitamins and said it was due to acidity. It took me seven days to recover fully. Members of staff at site took special care of me for which I am now thankful to them.

Shri B.M. Agrawal of Agrawal oil Mills Bhusawal

As I had earlier written that many people from Bhusawal were visiting the site out of their curiosity to know the development. One Shri Brijmohan Agrawal of 'Agrawal Oil Mills' Bhusawal visited the site during my illness. He met me for few minutes and introduced himself. Later when the mill started production he used to invite me regularly. One day laughingly, while giving the reference of his first visit, he told that he had never expected to see me again as he thought I would run away rather than staying in such conditions.

Mr. Bhatia visited the site. He too liked to stay with me in my room. Engineers discussed various matters of importance with him. I remember that the meeting always ended late in night. We had created a campfire atmosphere. Though the work might not have progressed well due to rains and many other reasons but he saw happiness on the faces of the staff members and their enthusiasm towards the work. He might have reported the matter to M.D.

Next time when M.D. K.K. Babu came to visit the site, engineers saw him smiling. They told me that they had after a long time seen him smiling. Though he was staying in Bhusawal in a rented house, he liked to take lunch with us at site. I have already written about him that he was a man who had kept his needs to bare minimum.

In the month of September 1981 Mr. P.K. Chopra a paper technologist who was appointed for this project and was stationed at Nasik joined us at site. He came with his wife and 6-month-old daughter Pooja. He was allotted one room. I was worried how he would stay with his family in such conditions. He never made any complaint. On the contrary he and his wife became source of encouragement for others. I could pass my time with this little doll. I remember that the quality of our food also improved, as one lady was there to supervise. The kitchen was more clean.

Mr. Makwana known as kakaji and his team returned from England after dismantling and dispatching the Paper Machine.

Months passed and fury of rains gradually started reducing. In October we received electricity connection. Engineers and contractors started working late night. Main factory building started gaining height. People who were suspicious started visiting the factory.

All the political leaders of Bhusawal and nearby areas were very helpful. Shri J.T.Mahajan who was the chairman of Madukar Sahakari Sakhar Karkana and M.L.A regularly visited the site. He assured me his full-fledged co-operation. Later he became Home Minister of Maharashtra.

Shri J.T Mahajan on a round of the factory under construction

SHRI MADHUKARRAO CHAUDHARI

Shri Madhukarrao Chaudhari who was the senior most leader of this area also visited the factory site. He had been minister for over 16 years and the most honest and respected leader of the area. He too visited the site. This was the biggest factory in his district of Jalgaon in size as well as in investment. I had maintained good relations with them and in turn all the authorities of district helped me.

K.G.Gupta garlanding Shri Chaudhari Saheb

In June 1982 shipment of Machinery was received and it was immediately to be sent to site. I do remember that we received over 100 trucks during July. We worked continuously 24 hours, as truck drivers were not ready to wait till morning. Sometimes truck divers came to the site in the middle of night with news that their truck was stuck on the road. Immediately we would send people carrying jacks, chain pulley block and ropes with them to bring the truck to factory. There were no lights along the entire length of 8 km of the road. We had therefore purchased many petromax for such emergencies. Here I would appreciate the dedication of Kakaji who despite being 52 years or age would accompany his team and work through the night in pouring rain.

From September 1982 work on erection of the Paper Machine began. The building work was almost 70% complete. Erection of Machine and construction of Building were going in parallel as we now had received full power. Erection work started with full swing. We also started employing skilled workers such as machine operators, boiler operators, fitters, welders and electricians etc. Here Mr. Khan helped me. I am at a loss of words for praising him. He had kept the record so accurate that no irregularity took place in appointments and no one questioned me. We, while acquiring the land had agreed o give appointment to the wards of landowners. They had given the names, which were noted down in a register bearing my signature at the time of acquisition of land in 1978. That register was well preserved by Mr. Khan.

CONSTRUCTION
OF LABOUR QUARTERS

I suggested K.K. Babu for construction of some quarters for labour and junior staff. He agreed to my proposal. I started construction of 50 labour quarters; ten in each row having common wall and asbestos roof were constructed. No one hesitated to stay in such quarter as we senior staff members were already staying in such quarters inside factory area. I also constructed 20 junior staff quarters having two bedrooms, hall, kitchen and self contained toilets and allotted to engineers and technical and administrative staff. Now we were ready for commissioning of the machine.

Building work was completed and erection of machine was in full speed.

However one serious shortcoming came to my notice. Erection of boiler was not gaining speed. Boiler engineer Mr. Kale was giving me false assurances. I got suspicious about his ability. Kakaji also told me about the slow speed of work at Boiler. One day when I was sitting in my office one Boiler operator Abdul Rehman came to see me. He informed me that Mr. Kale does not know much about boilers and if we do not take remedial action the boiler will never be erected. Next day I left for Nasik to discuss the matter with Boiler Inspector.

He also confirmed the apprehension of Kakaji. He also gave me the name of a contractor who could complete the work. The contractor was in Jalgaon. I appointed the contractor for boiler work. I also asked Mr. Kale to resign. I do not remember now how I came in contact with Shri V.P.Chaudhari who had worked in many factories as boiler engineer and was a resident of Bhusawal. I appointed him as boiler engineer. He completed the job and had the boiler ready before the erection of machine. He was an asset for the mills. Later when we undertook the training and improvement of skills program I made it a point to see that at least two engineers should be trained as proficiency engineer and three boiler operators as first class boiler operators. Mr. V.P. Chaudhari appeared for the proficiency engineer examination. I Issued necessary certificate required for appearing in examination without fearing that they may leave the company after passing examination. Mr. Ashok Parmar, son in law of Kakaji, was a mechanical engineer. I transferred him to boiler department under Shri V.P.Chaudhari. I insisted that he should also appear for the proficiency engineer's exam and issued necessary experience certificate to him. He too passed the exam in first attempt. Shri Abdul Rehman and Shri S.D Patil also appeared for first class boiler examination and became successful. This was done somewhere in 1985. I would also write few lines at appropriate time and place.

INAUGURATION

On 26 January 1983 we started the Paper Machine. Shri Madhukar Raoji Chaudhari did the Inauguration. All the family members of Somani family came to the Factory. Arrangement of their stay was made in the Guesthouse of Deepnagar power House. This power house and our factory was divided by river Tapi. They all came in morning and returned in evening.

SHRI S.B.BHUTADA

It took one more month to complete all the alignments. Regular production was started by the end of March of 1983. All the distributors were appointed. They appreciated the quality of paper. I wanted one local dealer. No one had approached for dealership from district Jalgaon. One day along with my driver I reached Jalgaon and met Mr. S.B. Bhutada who was in the paper business. He was a qualified mechanical engineer and had worked in paper factories of repute. He was also an old employee of Somani's. He was also well known to me. I had met him in Calcutta during my tenure there. I insisted that he become the distributor. He was hesitant. I told him that I intend to deliver first truck of our paper in Jalgaon and I do not consider any one reliable other than him. He agreed on my insistence. I agreed to his suggestion of paying security deposit in installments. The first truckload material was dispatched to him on 23rd March 1983.

Later when production and quality stabilized he would come to me, many times, for special sanction of material over his quota or for early manufacturing of his requirement. Many times we would laugh together when I would remind him that one day I had approached him and now he was approaching me. Now Mr. Bhutada is of 83 years of age and still very active. He is now owner of a kraft paper mill. I recently met him. We still laugh remembering those days.

SHRI P.K.CHOPRA

During these two months of alignment I concentrated on appointment of necessary technical staff for paper machine and finishing house. Shri P.K. Chopra was having excellent contacts in many paper mills. Some people, who had earlier worked with him, sent their application. I had to simply issue appointment orders. In fact he also prepared orders. My signature was only a formality. It became an open fact. Everyone believed that Mr. P.K.Chopra was controlling all the activities of mills. I too did not try to erase this impression. I knew that Mr. Chopra was a dedicated and honest person who had made extraordinary sacrifices. I have already mentioned that he had come at site with his newly wed wife, a 6-month-old daughter and stayed in temporary rooms. He never complained about any lack of facility.

The mill started functioning smoothly. There were some small problems here and there but all the political leaders and district authorities were in favour of the mill being the largest in Jalgaon district, so no one wanted to disturb us.

ERECTION OF PULP MILLS

By the end of 1983 work of erection of pulp mills and installation of 2nd boiler was taken in hand. For pulp mills three 18 feet diameter digesters were to be fabricated and erected. I had earlier mentioned that K.K. Babu was himself an engineer therefore he liked to undertake the work departmentally. All the drawings and designs were finalized and the work was handed over to Shri Makwanaji (kakaji). Though no engineering degree was attached to his name he was a karma yogi. He constructed and erected the digester by the end of 1984.

As far as second Boiler is concerned most reliable boiler engineer Shri V.P.Chaudhari had assured me that the work will be completed before the erection of digesters. He kept his promise.

However here boiler inspector informed me to appoint at least one proficiency engineer and three first class boiler operators. I requested him to give me some time. He expressed his inability, as this was the legal requirement. I gave advertisement in newspaper. While we received some applications no one showed his inclination to stay at the site. One first class boiler operator who was a resident of nearby village and working in some other paper mill wanted to return near to his village. I appointed him. His name was S.W.Patil. He was attending to the boiler in all the three shifts for an hour in each shift. Abdul Rehman and other boiler operator S.D.Patil who were second class boiler operators were very reliable and experienced. By this time Mr. Parmar was also transferred by me to the boiler department. I again discussed the matter with boiler inspector who had a very practical attitude. He advised me to ask Shri V.P. Chaudhari to appear for the Proficiency Engineer Examination and other two Boiler Operator viz Abdul Rehman and S.D.Patil for first class boiler operators. I called all of them one by one. All of them informed me that though they are having necessary experience no one in previous management was ready to give them the certificate of experience as the management was afraid of their leaving the job after acquiring the qualification. I gave the necessary certificates to all of them and they passed in first attempt. Mr. Parmar too appeared for the examination and passed the exam in the first attempt in 1985. They remained in service without any complaint till I left the job in December 1990 and afterwards too.

SANJAY DHARDE

It will not be out of context to mention the case of Shri Sanjay Dharde. He had a B.Sc degree and had completed articleship necessary to appear in Chartered Accountants Examination. He applied for a job in accounts department. I appointed him as Accounts Assistant. Later I realized that he is holding a degree of B.Sc therefore it will be difficult for me to promote him in Finance Department. Further I would not be able to shift him in to laboratory, as he has no experience of technical nature. One day when I was sitting without any work I called him and put before him this fact and asked why he did not complete his course. He told me that it was because of his financial condition. He asked my advice. I advised him to appear for the Chartered Accountants Examination. I offered him to grant leave for six months. This offer did not work. He told me that without salary he will not be able to support himself. His father and mother had died in his childhood. Though he was a bachelor but he had to support his brother and sister. I agreed to grant six months leave with pay before examination and gave him light work for studies. He started preparing himself for Intermediate examination and before six months of examination proceeded on leave. He appeared for the examination and joined his duties. Result was declared when he was at work. He was declared successful. Now problem with me was how to grant him leave with pay again. If I discuss this matter with K.K Babu I will have to accept that I had granted leave with pay earlier. That too without his sanction. Without discussing the matter with him I was not gathering courage to grant leave with pay. One mistake could be condoned but repeated mistakes may be considered breach of trust. One day when K.K. Babu visited factory I put Mr. Dharde's case before him. I remember he smiled. Perhaps he knew that I had earlier granted him 6 months leave with pay. Without saying a word he immediately sanctioned leave with pay but advised me to enter into an agreement so that Mr. Dharde serves the company for three years after passing examination. Mr. Dharde agreed and he was granted leave. He appeared and passed the examination. He completed three years agreement and then left India to serve in East Africa. He is now a well-established practicing chartered accountant and practicing in Nasik. He often meets me. I think God had wished me to become a carrier in shaping his future.

SHRI ARUN SOMANI

Second is the case of Shri Arun Somani who was working as Accounts Officer with me in the factory. He was an extra-ordinary intelligent person. His memory was very sharp. One day he came to me and informed me that he wanted to leave the job and start business. I was shocked. I was not willing to leave such a useful person. I asked him if he wanted any raise. He declined all my offers and said that he was no more interested in service. He wanted to start a business. He submitted his resignation letter. I again called him and said that his letter of resignation will be kept with me. If at any time he decides to join service he would first come to me. He agreed. I did not accept his resignation and granted leave without pay for record purpose and kept the letter with me. I do not know why he changed his mind after 5 months and asked me over telephone if he could join again. I agreed. K.K. Babu was also informed about this matter. He was the person who had seen many such cases in his life. He was also having respect for good and dedicated persons. He was happy with this development.

Today Arun Somani is working as Joint General Manager in one of the cement factories of Birlas. His younger brother is a practicing Chartered Accountant in Nasik, looking after my financial matters and is a Secretary of my Charitable Trust in which I run an English Medium High School. I am really proud of them and happy to have association with them.

SHRI HANUMANSINGH GAHLOT

Earlier I had written about him. I was having a soft corner for him. When I was in Nasik Shri Motisingh Chauhan, who had trained me, referred him to me. His daughter Pinki and two school-going sons were very much attached to me. My wife had regarded him as her younger brother. He truly discharged the onus of that relationship. I stayed alone in Dushkheda for 5 years. He became my caretaker. I am thankful to him for taking care of me in those days. Later in May 2001 the marriage of his daughter Pinki was solemnized in the hall of my house and she was given a send off from my house at Nasik.

LEVA PATILS COMMUNITY

Here I would also like to add few lines about my experience of Leva Patils. This is a community settled in the villages in and around District Jalgaon. They are very honest and laborious peoples, dedicated to work. My success and the running of mills smoothly were mainly because of the contribution made by this community. Shri Madhukarraoji Chaudhari, Shri J.T.Mahajan and Dr.Gunvantrao Sarode resident of Savada and a member of parliament were the leaders from this community.

SHRI V. SHESHADRIRAO

Fabrication of digestors for pulpmill was in full speed and other equipment had arrived at the site and had been installed. We lacked a person with experience in pulp mill operations. During erection of digestors Mr. Darak, chief executive of West coast paper mills visited with Mr. Misal who was working as Asst. General Manager (Pulp). He had many years of experience in operation of pulp mill and was considered to be one of the best technical people in paper mills. He inspected the erection work and submitted his report in which he recommended the appointment of pulp mill manager immediately. Mr. Darak also invited me to West coast paper mills. He arranged my visit to three efficient paper mills. I had seen West coast paper mills and Andhra Pradesh paper mills earlier many times in connection with paper requirement of ISP when I was in Nasik. Mr Misal accompanied me to Sheshasai Paper mills on the bank of Kaveri, Tamil Nadu Newsprint and Mysore pulp and paper mills. I gained some idea about pulp mill. Then he recommended the name of Shri V. Sheshadrirao who was working as works manager (Pulp) in Mandya National paper mills Mysore. K.K. Babu asked me to meet Mr. Rao personally and if possible persuade him to join our mill. It was a difficult task. First he was a government employee who seldom switches over the job in private sector. Second, the working culture was different. Third and most important was that he was a resident of Mysore a place just 15 km away from Mandya National Paper Mill.

I reached Mysore. I think Mr. Misal had already sounded him about my visit. I met him in Mysore at his residence. He was a typical type of south Indian Brahmin, a forthright person. He had clear, commanding and strong voice. He enjoyed giving lectures. He gave a good lecture on pulp mill for about 45 minutes. It was my first impression that he was an academician. He arranged my visit to Mandya National paper mills. He also showed me Brindavan Gardens, which is just about a few kilometers from Mandya National. I explained to him purpose of my visit and requested him to think about the proposal. I also told him that I would like to finalize the matter during my visit itself. Therefore if he is inclined to join us we could discuss his conditions. I agreed to meet him next day. When next day I went to his house, without any formality he informed me about his inclination to accept my proposal. He was very straightforward person and told me that he did not know how to negotiate. He gave me a sheet of paper on which he had written all his conditions. Without taking much time after reading I conveyed my acceptance to all of his conditions. I asked him if he had any further condition to add he may do so. He was surprised and asked me if I did not need the sanction of M.D. I informed him that M.D trusted my decisions and never questioned any one of such decisions in past. He was impressed with my confidence. I asked again finally if he wanted any other condition to add. Now it was his turn to believe in my honesty. He told me that he considered me a friend and requested me to add conditions that he might have forgotten. I added the refund of all the expenses for shifting his residence from Mysore to Duskheda. He agreed that as soon as he received the letter of offer he would resign from his present job. He also informed me that he would have to give one month's notice.

On reaching Dushkheda the first thing I did was to issue the letter of offer to him. He on receipt informed me that he had submitted his resignation. After one month he joined us in the year 1984.

He was about 10 years elder to me. He was a pious man. Every day morning for about one hour he will recite mantras from Vedas. On the first day of his joining I introduced him to all the members of staff. I said jokingly that if you have minimum 30 minutes of time then only go to his cabin to see him. At that time they could not understand. Mr. Rao clarified that he had given lecture to me every time I met him. He spoke in Hindi in typical type of south Indian accent "Dekho bhai ham to Brahmin admi hay aur toda bolne ka adat jasti hai". Later I asked about their experience with him.

Everyone was happy to work with such an openhearted man. His wife was a good singer and by nature a good woman. She had better knowledge of Hindi. She soon became friendly with all the families staying in the colony.

He maintained equilibrium with Mr. P.K. Chopra who was working as production manager. He knew that Mr. Chopra is considered as the right hand man of General Manager though this was not the reason. Mr. Chopra though was the youngest manager but was a very matured person. He always gave good advice.

Mr. Rao was also a very sweet person. If he wanted to get any work done from his assistant against his wish he will always say" I am not asking you to do this work as works manager but as an elderly man."

Many times when he was in good mood enjoying hard drinks in a party with me he would say in his typical south Indian Hindi accent "Gupta sahib tum G.M. hogamagar ham tum se umar me bada hay is liye tumkolecture deta rahega (Mr Gupta you may be the G.M. but I am elder in age to you therefore I will always lecture you).

In 1988 he was promoted as Deputy General Manager and Mr Chopra as Assistant General Manager.

When I left the job in 1990 he was promoted as General Manger and Mr. Chopra took the rein from him as General Manger after his retirement in 1995.

After his retirement I met him in Mysore when his daughter Aparna was getting married and once again in the year 2008. He died in the year 2011. I still have his sweet memories and would never forget a jolly good fellow.

SHRI P.K. CHOPRA AND HIS THREE MUSKETEERS

I had written earlier about Mr. Chopra and would be writing whenever any reference about his contribution comes. He was the person who had longest stay with the mill. He joined us in 1981 and left the mill in 2000.

Three persons were his most faithful lieutenants. Mr. P.J.Mathew, Shri Akhlesh Sharma and Shri B.N.Jha. All these three were quite young. Mr. Mathew was from Kerala. He was soft spoken. Due to his little knowledge of Hindi he could not communicate a lot with workers. He would take instructions from Mr. Chopra to plan the production. He was responsible for the quality of paper. Mr. Akhilesh Sharma and Mr. B.N.Jha were quite young and fierce persons. Both were holding important positions. Akhilesh was paper Machine In charge and Jha babu was finishing house In charge. All the three were commanding 60% of the most important labour force of the factory. All these three were very dedicated boys. To disturb Akhilesh meant loss of production. To disturb Jha babu meant loss of finished goods for dispatch. Akhilesh was dealing with paper machine operators. Whenever I was on round and if a paper sheet was broken he would run from one end of the machine to other end shouting on operators instructing them to run and attend the problematic area. He will forget my presence and hurled abuses in air fluently. He was afraid of his most trusted friend

Jha Babu, who would complain about non-availability of paper for finishing. Jha babu was dealing with 40 Finishers who are considered most troublemakers. Often we use to call Jha babu as 'Ali Baba with his 40 thieves'. Since local skilled workers were not available Jha babu had all the Bihari finishers. Jha babu himself was from Bihar. If sometimes I wanted some material on priority basis I would have to request him. He told me me that to understand the mentality of Bihari workers was difficult for me and therefore I should allow him only to deal with them. Perhaps he was not aware that when I worked in Calcutta 60% of working force was Bihari. Though it was because of the excellent planning of Mr. Rao and Mr. Chopra but these three people on shop floor were equally responsible for our receiving Productivity award in 1985 and more awards thereafter. Akhilesh Sharma is at present executive director of a paper mills in Vapi and meets me frequently whenever I go there to see my Nephew. I met Mr. Mathew in 2009 while travelling with my friends from Munnar to Kochi. He invited me to his house and arranged a lunch for all of us in a Hotel with bottles of beer. We remembered old days. He holds a very important position in a paper mill in Kerala. However I have lost contact with Shri B.N.Jha. I have heard from Mr. Chopra that he is in Calcutta and well settled.

DAYARAM DEVRAM SONAWANE

Before I proceed further I would like to mention about this boy. In the year 1983 when we started production I faced one difficulty. Boiler ash, which we had anticipated would result in some earning by way of sale, did not materialize. On the contrary I had to spend money for its removal in order to keep the boiler area clean. I advertised in local newspaper for its sale, but nobody turned up. Generally brick makers use boiler ash. I was told that our boiler ash contained more khangars (coal which is over burnt). After few months a person from Bhusawal approached me. By that time I had started giving it free of cost. He started taking the boiler ash. I saved at least on account of expenses on its removal. Later I realized that it was a mistake on my part. The person who was taking it free did not allow anyone to approach me.

During this time one boy Dayaram Devram Sonavane a resident of Dushkheda village approached me. His age might have been 25 years. He wanted a job in factory as unskilled worker. In those days wage of unskilled worker was Rs. 600 to Rs. 700. I was not able to give him the job as he was not a landowner whose land was acquired for factory purpose. I discussed with him about his source of income and activities. He was married and having dependent parents. He was having a small piece of land but the income from agricultural activity was not sufficient to support family. He told me very frankly that he was distilling illicit liquor for additional income. Sometimes he earned but most of the times during police raid he lost heavily and had to remain in police custody.

Police after destroying their material and equipment kept them 4 to 5 days in custody and then allowed them to leave. It was a known fact that these people did not have any other work to support their families and were compelled to adopt this work. There were approximately 20 to 25 other people who along Tapti River bank in ravines were carrying on this work. I saw helplessness on his face. I saw in him a person who wanted to adopt a life of an honest man but due to compelling circumstances was walking on a wrong road. I called him next day. On that day in the evening during introspection I thought about him. I think God also wanted through me to reform these boys. An idea crept in my mind. Next day again he came to see me in my office. I called him at my residence in evening when I could discuss my plans with him at leisure.

He came to my residence. I told him frankly that I could not give him any type of permanent employment in factory. But I would see that he gets Rs1000 per month. He agreed. At that time I had promised 50 truckloads of coal ash to the person who was taking it free of cost. Out of this he had already taken 40 truckload material. After giving 10 more truckload material I stopped the delivery of boiler ash to him. He did not say a word on the contrary boasted outside that the management with folded hands would call him. In the mean time I had asked Dayaram to find out where this person was selling the material. He found out that the man kept the material at

Bhusawal from where he would sell it to brick makers. I asked Dayaram to lift the material from Boiler and keep some if he had the place. Since he did not have such a place I gave him a place inside the factory. He started removing the ash from boiler. I advanced him the amount of labour charges plus Rs.1000/—PM as his remuneration. After three months when the stock of earlier person was exhausted brick makers started enquiring from Dayaram. He faced another difficulty that he was not having any transport to carry the material up to brick makers site. I advanced money to purchase a second hand Truck. He started removing the ash. I fixed Rs.10 per brass that came to Rs 30 per truck.

By the end of May I recovered the full money I had advanced to him. Thereafter I gradually increased the price every year. He too started taking ash directly from boiler to a place outside the factory for storing. He had taken a piece of agricultural land on a rental basis. In due course he purchased that piece of land. It was his first purchase. Later I was told that he accumulated many acres of land. He had employed almost all the persons who were earlier carrying on the work of illicit distillation. These persons were very hard workers. They were truck drivers, mechanics and very stout people suitable for hard work. In 1984 when we started 2 boiler and pulp mills he was well settled in this business having added two more trucks. He also solved my difficulty of removing pulp sludge, which we were storing in lagoons outside factory compound on the river bank. I was always worried that due to heavy rains it may find its way in the river. Pumping station of Bhusawal water works was down stream on the Tapti River. I called him again. Mr. Bhutda and Mr. Chopra informed me that this sludge can be utilized by persons making sun dried board. Dayaram contacted them and started removing sludge from lagoons. He along with his boys proved to be an asset to me. By the end of 1985 villagers started addressing him "Dayaram Seth" as a mark of their respect for him.

He helped me to maintain good relation with the villagers. One day he took K. K. Babu to his village. They did not have any facility of drinking water. All the villagers used to carry water from the River. K. K. Babu agreed to provide drinking water. We laid a 1.5 km pipeline from our water clarification plant to his village. In the year 1990 when I left the services to start my own business, he was well settled. Having sufficient agricultural land and an office just opposite the residential colony of our mills. Later I heard that he was elected as a member of Jillah Parishad of Dist. Jalgoan. He also opened a primary school in his village that has been recognized by Government and now getting sufficient aid. Unfortunately he had not taken due care of his health. He died in the year 2008. This is a story of a person who was instrumental in transforming the life, of the boys whom we the people of civilized society call "Rogues". It is the true story of reform of 25 boys. The police inspector of that area who was close to me also praised Dayaram many times in my presence. I could not resist my temptation to give him full two pages in my story as he was a self made person. If given a proper chance and support these village boys can make any business successful.

CHILDREN OF COLONY

In the year 1985 there were nearly 30 children in the age group of 2 to 4 years. All the children of the colony were addressing me as "Bade Uncle". They were very friendly with me. I used to keep chocolates in my pocket to give them. Many of them had free entry in my house even in my absence. As I was staying alone they were my past time. One Sunday evening I purchased about 100 lollypops from the colony grocery shop and planted in my garden silently and went inside the house. After some time one child came to my house and saw lollypops standing in my garden. The news that "Bade uncle" has grown lollypops in his garden spread like wildfire. All the children of the colony were excited and assembled near my garden. I allowed each of them to take two lollypops. Later they always asked me when I would plant next time.

Chemical recovery boiler and my Europe tour

Under the able leadership of K.K. Babu the mill was making a sturdy progress. He always gave importance to cost control. He completed the project well within projected figures. We were making sufficient profit to undertake expansion every year. We had already erected and commissioned pulp mill. It started generating black liquor, which had every possibility to pollute Tapi River water. We therefore planned to erect a recovery boiler to solve the problem of black liquor.

K.K Babu located a second hand recovery plant in Sweden. It was decided to send a team for dismantling and dispatch of plant to India. Shri Makwana was ready with his a team and under his leadership the team was to be sent to Sweden. K.K. Babu had promised me a Europe tour with my wife if the mill becomes a profitable venture. He asked me to go with them and settle them in Delery a village near Stockholm the capital city of Sweden. After settling them I could start my Europe tour. It was his kind gesture. I had written earlier that he was a person who always kept his promises. I was not a technical person even then I was sent as a leader of the team to settle them and hand over the leadership to Kakaji later. My elder son Sundeep had appeared for 12th examination. I asked him if his mom could take a tour of Europe with me. He agreed to take care of Amit. A maidservant Jamuna Bai was there in my

Nasik house and used to live with us as a family member. She had joined us when I came to Nasik in 1974.

At that time her age was 19 years. She was suffering from Polio in one leg therefore she decided not to marry. She had taken care of both my children since they were very young. They also treated her with respect. Therefore there was no problem for my wife to accompany me on the tour. I along with nearly 20 people, left India on 30th May 1985. From Stockholm our agent took us to Delery. He had already arranged a villa for our stay. We had taken a cook also in our team. Mrs. Makwana was also in the team. My wife and Mrs. Makwana arranged kitchen and helped cook for few days. When the team was well settled I with my wife started my tour.

I had already written in my childhood memories that I had read many novels. The writers of many countries wrote them, including France, Germany, Denmark, Sweden, England, Italy, Spain, in short almost all the countries of Europe. Literature is the mirror of society. I was anxious to see the inside of these countries. It was possible only if I travel by train because sky is the same everywhere. I therefore purchased Euro-rail pass for 30 days and started from Delery. I came to Copenhagen the capital of Denmark. From there I wanted to travel by train to England. It was my mistake, as I did not have a visa for Germany, Luxembourg and Belgium. I was deported back from Germany to Denmark in the night at 2 am. From Denmark I purchased a ticket by a ship for England. It took me to England by sea. I enjoyed my travel in North Sea. Many oil tankers run in North Sea. It looked lighted as if many cars were running on the road.

From the seaport of England I travelled by train to London. After staying few days in London and traveling nearby areas by car. I left for France by train. My onward journeys were all by train. From France to Italy to Switzerland back to Italy. I visited Spain, as I wanted to see the windmills and bull fight. From there I again came to France and England and back to Sweden via Amsterdam. I had read the diary of Anne Frank therefore visited her house in Amsterdam. From Stockholm I travelled to Norway. I do not want this writing to become a lengthy one giving details of the places visited, therefore I stop here.

SUNDEEP AGAIN

I returned to Bombay on 7ᵗʰ July 1985. I was keeping contact with my sons over telephone during journey. I was worried about Sundeep's result of 12ᵗʰ standard examination and his admission to a good engineering college. When one day I telephoned him from Paris he informed me that he has cleared the examination with good marks and was planning to go to BITS Pilani for admission. He wanted to pursue his studies in Electronics subject. BITS Pilani was teaching this subject. When I came to Nasik he informed me that he had sought admission in BITS Pilani. When I saw his Mark sheet I came to know that he had stood 7ᵗʰ in the Merit list of Pune Board and secured 93% overall and 97.4% in PCM. He had not informed me this fact over telephone. Mrs. Sunder his teacher about whom I had mentioned earlier was very happy. I also thanked her and her children Niki and Nina who had played an important role in the development of my both the sons.

Now since Sundeep was to go to college hostel at Pilani. I transferred my younger son Amit and his mother to Bhusawal. Sundeep also came to Bhusawal as his college was to start from July. Lions club of Bhusawal felicitated him for his outstanding performance in HSC examination and securing 7ᵗʰ place in the Merit list.

DEVELOPMENT OF COLONY

By this time the colony had fully developed. We had constructed senior staff quarters and Manager quarters. A guesthouse consisting of 15 rooms, kitchen and dining room was also constructed. A community hall, which could accommodate 200 people, was also ready. Our administrative office was also ready.

TRANSFER OF CHILDREN TO NASIK FOR EDUCATION

Amit was doing fairly well, so far as his studies were concerned, in Nasik. It was my mistake to transfer him to Dushkheda. He was admitted in 9th Standard in St. Aloysius convent high school a English medium school at Bhusawal. The Company purchased a school bus. Many other children studying in different schools at Bhusawal were travelling in this bus. By the year-end it was evident that he was not going to adjust there. He was asking me to transfer him to Nasik. In the new academic year in 1986 he gave me a final notice that he would not go to school unless he was transferred to Nasik. Sending him to Nasik would result in sending his mother too. I would have to stay alone again. However it so happened that Mr. Rao's daughter Aparna passed 10th and two sons of our chief engineer Shri R.K.Mhaeshwari too passed 10th and 8th standard. The name of the elder one was Shailendra and younger was Anurag. There was no good college at Bhusawal and district place Jalgaon was 45 km away from Dushkeda. Though they would have got the admission in good college at Jalgaon but it would have been difficult to go up and down to that place.

During my program of introspection I thought over this problem. An idea came to my mind. Why not to shift Amit, Aparna, Shailendra and Anurag to Nasik to my house. The house was quite big with four bedrooms, a big hall and a kitchen. My maidservant Jamunabai was staying alone there. Next day I had a family dinner with Mr. Rao, and Mr. R.K.Maheshwari in presence of these children. I suggested that all of them should be sent to Nasik. My house was in the center of the city. College and school were at the walking distance. I told them house was already lying vacant and a maidservant was also living there. I had retained and was paying remuneration to elder sister of Jamunabai who was cleaning utensils and flooring. I suggested that all these children could stay comfortably there for their further studies. I also suggested that for every 15 days one of the mothers would go to Nasik and stay with them. This way the children will get home cooked food and would be able to continue studies and would not feel absence of their mother. Everyone liked this idea. Children shouted "Hurrah" as their consent. I sent all of them in June 1986 to Nasik and my wife stayed with them till they were settled. As the house was already lying vacant, I had retained both the servants and was already paying them so I decided to share only kitchen expenses, which were hardly 200 to 300 per child. Aparna was happy to eat north Indian food where as other boys enjoyed south Indian cuisine. Jamuna Bai also learned how to prepare South Indian breakfast. This way the children continued for 2 years till they completed their higher secondary exam.

After completing their education at Nasik Amit sought admission in a Engineering college at Pune named as MIT, Aparna went to Banglore and did B.Sc in Botany, Biochemistry and Microbiology at Mysore University from 1988-1991 and M.Sc in Biochemistry from 1991-1993 at North Maharashtra

University, Jalgaon. Shailendra to B.J medical college at Pune and Anurag to R.K.MET engineering college-Nagpur. All these children are well settled now. Aparna at present is staying at Banglore and helping her husband in his business. Shailendra is a Doctor in Hinduja hospital at Mumbai.Anurag is in Pune having his own business. Amit is in USA as a software Engineer.

After settling them in Nasik 1986 all the three families viz mine, Shri R.K.Maheshwari our chief Engineer and Shri S.B.Bhutada made a program to visit Kedarnath, Gangotri, Jamnotri and Badrinath. We enjoyed our trip.

In 1989 Sundeep completed his Engineering course and decided to proceed to U.S.A for further studies. He completed his M.S in engineering from University of Missouri and subsequently a Management Science degree from Stanford University.

SHRI. VINODCHANDRA C. PAREKH

In the year 1987 Shri. Vinodbhai Parekh a Gujrati gentleman came to Bhusawal to meet me at Shri Vindya Paper Mills. When he came to me with Mr.K.D. Parekh, our Marketing Manager, he had received a supply order for 1500 Tons of paper from Government of Madhya Pradesh. The entire order was to be completed within one month. He had filled the tender on very competitive rates subject to payment that was to be made to them within 15 days. He negotiated the price with us and demanded cash discount of 3% if the payment was made within 15 days. Our management agreed. The entire material was to be supplied by us within one month. He came to Bhusawal with his son Hareshbhai. He discussed with me the probable difficulties that could be faced in supply of material. He wanted continuous run of machine till 1500 Tons paper is produced. I agreed to his condition but told him that he will have to arrange the truck transport. He agreed. A date was fixed for production. Before one day he came with his three employees. He posted one at Jalgaon a district place where trucks were available. The Job of that person was to hire trucks and see that at any rate entire material manufactured is dispatched on the same day. The job of second person was to coordinate with production people so that the required quality and quantity is produced. Third person will take the bill and documents in the evening after dispatch of material and rush to Bhopal the capital of state of Madhya Pradesh to handover the documents to their representative who in turn will submit the documents and arrange the release of payment within time. Thus one man was coordinating, other was arranging trucks and third person was making a daily trip up and down to Bhopal. This way he completed the order of 1500 MT in one month. Made the payment to us in 15 days thereby earned Rs 900 per ton on 1500 tons a total amount of Rs.13,50000/ (1.35 million) by way of cash discount. He also earned Rs 1000/per ton by way of price difference. Thus in one month he earned 28.50 lacs (2.85 million) that too without investing a single rupee from his own pocket. Later he became very friendly with me and informed me that the same way he had completed a supply order of 4000 Tons paper purchased from Rayalseema Paper Mills within two months and earned over a crore (Ten Million) of Rupees without investing a single rupee from his pocket. I was greatly impressed by this gentleman. When one day we both were sitting in the evening over dinner he informed me that he started his career as a professor in Oriental Languages in a degree College at Kolhapur. Later he left the job and shifted to Bombay where he took L.L.B. degree. From Bombay he shifted to Ahmedabad and he joined a modest paper business of his father-in—law Shri. Maneklal Desai who was a generous, honest, a daring man, and ardent follower of Gandhiji. During freedom movement Shri Maneklal Desai went to jail. He was more devoted to social service. Vinodbhai took over his business and gave him freedom to devote himself to social work. He shifted to his native village to devote full time in more meaningful social work.

Getting a free hand Vinodbhai expanded his business multifold procuring almost over a dozen wholesale dealerships and building them into largest, prestigious business under the original title Kalyan paper Mart. Because of his studies and prominence in business, he was elected to be the President of Paper Merchants Association, Ahmedabad for 15 years in succession. Later in 1991, he was elected to be the President of the Federation of Pater Traders Association (FPTA). His work was appreciated and he was bestowed with all the honours open for President ship—the crowning glory of his life.

I heard him carefully. He told me that before accepting any supply order he cautiously draws a planned strategy to complete it. I watched his way of doing business vigilantly out of curiosity. I never expected that this experience will help me in future because it was a remote possibility for me to leave such a lucrative job and start my own business. But when I started my business after leaving services of Shri Vindhya Paper mills and received sizable orders from Government departments I adopted the same policy and completed thousands of tons of order without any investment.

He had become a business idol for me. When my son Sundeep was completing his degree from BITS Pilani he had to complete a project. He stayed for two months with this family in 1988 and completed his project in Space Application Center (SAC) Ahmedabad. When he came to me I found a complete change in him. He was all the time praising this family and way of working of Vinod bhai Parekh. As a mark of my respect I thought it proper to write a few lines about this outstanding businessman whose teaching enabled me to draw my business strategy and become successful in my business venture.

LABOUR UNREST AND LOCKOUT

In 1988 Recovery Boiler shipments were received from Sweden. However by October 1988 labour unrest started. Though I agreed to most of their demands they kept submitting new demands one after other. Since the last two years I was paying them bonus @20%, P.F was also introduced. Company had purchased a retirement plan from LIC for all its employees. Still they were not satisfied. They joined the union of Dr. Datta Samant a well-known labour leader of Bombay. I knew that if I recognize his union it will be the end of paper mill. I did not recognize that union, as a result workers resorted to violence. It was on 24th November 1988 in the evening. On that very day M.D was busy in the marriage of his daughter and when I telephoned him he was receiving the Barat. I informed him that I was declaring a lock out. He simply listened and advised me to take whatever action I deemed fit. I declared the lock out. During that lock out striking workers arranged a meeting of Dr. Samant in a field just opposite to factory. Apart from workers their family members also attended the meeting. The meeting was at 5 pm. People started gathering since 3 pm. Many people from nearby village were eager to see the famous Dr. Samant. I had given the information about the meeting to Collector of Jalgaon. He made elaborate arrangements so that any untoward incident did not take place. Dr. Samant did not attend the meeting. Instead his brother attended in his place. Later I came to know that due to his security reasons he declined to come to a remote village. That was the first sign that discouraged the villagers. The workers leaders in order to maintain the morale of workers announced another date and assured that Dr Samant himself would come. Within one month they announced two or three dates but the meeting did not take place. During this period I wrote three letters and circulated them amongst striking workers, villagers and local politicians. I explained about their demands and what we were paying. I also explained to workers that factory is just like a ship and during a storm if the ship sank, the first loss of life will be to workmen who are on the ship in open sea. Owners would suffer only financial loss. If the factory is closed no new investment would come to this remote village and prosperity that had come would vanish.

Villagers and politicians understood the facts. However workers tore the leaflets. I had expected this. They openly abused the local politicians. I had seen that skilled workers were losing their patience. The workers leaders were giving dates one after another about the visit of Dr. Samant thus boosting their morale. They invented fancy slogans and whole day shout these slogans in a field against our housing colony." Aadhi Roti Khayenge Datta Samant Layenge" (We will bring Datta Samant even if it means that we don't get a full meal). Children of my colony too without knowing the meaning would run here and there shouting such slogans. Now the striking workers only aim was to bring Dr Samant by all their might. Five of the workmen went to Bombay and called over the telephone to set the date on which Dr. Samant would visit.

District administration had put sufficient force around the factory. One company of State Reserve Police with 30 people and one Inspector was deployed for the safety of plant and machinery. Local police was also posted. District administration was also worried about the entry of Dr. Samant in Jalgaon. As I had written earlier that ours was the biggest factory. Once Dr. Samant got entry the industrial peace of whole district would have been jeopardized.

More than one month passed. I realised that this was not the usual strike of workers that take place in a city. In industrial belt worker are totally dependent on their wages. Here they were first agriculturist. They were working in paper mill for additional income. I realized that this way they would continue the strike for months.

I was an active member of Jalgaon district Industries Association. All the members were worried and watching my action. The Collector also had a meeting with me and wanted to know if I was going to accept their demands. I flatly refused and told him that it will be suicidal for the company and also other industries. He did not comment but clearly I saw a sign of relief on his face. Next day he provided more police protection for the safety of staff members who were living in colony.

Mr. J.C.Jain was the president, Mr.D.G.Muchrikar, Secretary and R.J Kothari was a very active member of Jalgaon Industries Association. They contacted every politician of the District and explained to them the facts of strike and management's point of view. They neglected their daily work and helped me out of the way. I am thankful to them. They contacted each and every influential person small or big and explained about the recent prosperity industrial development has brought in Jalgaon. They made dedicated efforts and provided facts and figures to these people. All the politicians understood the gravity of the situation and kept themselves aloof from the workers trying to bring Dr Samant. In fact one very influential politician Shri Suresh dada Jain assured me of his support over telephone. Shri Madhukar Raoji Chaudhari, Shri J.T Mahajan and Dr Gunvantrao Sarode an M.P also assured me of their support.

I made a group of our employees working in Labour department. They visited all the village heads of the villages from where workers used to come to work in paper mills. This group explained to them the facts of strike and why we do not want to negotiate with Dr Samant.

All these efforts turned the sympathy wave in our favour. Workers openly started abusing these people and declared them corrupt. Madhukar Roaji Chaudhari was a well known person. Every one knew that he was the most honest person. Abusing him annoyed the local people and politicians.

Now K.K. Babu was also worried but he did not disturb me in my fight. I told him not to visit the factory. Collector granted me a licence for holding weapon for security. I purchased an imported revolver. During all this time I stayed in colony. That was a moral support for staff members.

Now I had waited for sufficient time. My fighting spirit overpowered me. I discussed my plan with K.K. Babu. He agreed fully. I decided to start the factory. I lifted the lock out. As I had expected not a single worker came for work. They all laughed and started shouting fancy slogans more vociferously. They did not get any idea of my plan in reality.

Dayaram seth and his 25 to 30 people showed their inclination to work. Our security contractor Mr. Tiwari who was a ex service man also came and assured me that he could get about 200 workman from Itarsi about 200 km for Bhusawal a city of M.P. My main problem was of operation of boiler. If I started boiler with unskilled labour though in supervision of engineers, boiler inspector may order shutdown of boilers. I did not want to take any immature decision in hurry.

I have written earlier, several times whenever my fighting spirit gained control of me, some invisible power to whom I call God also helped me. One night Abdul Rehman and S.K.Patil two boiler operators came to my residence and assured me that they would join their duties. Third boiler supervisor Sardarji who was an excellent boiler operator was always with me, though his son Mohan who was working as welder had become the labour leader. Sardarji was with me in Nasik and I had helped him when he was seriously ill. I had kept him in company's guesthouse for three months with full pay. His only problem was his addiction to liquor. Therefore I was afraid to give him the independent charge of boiler operation. He promised me that he would not drink during the days of strike and I am happy to say here that he kept his promise. This was a great opportunity for me to move and take a bold decision. Ismail Wahab also met me and assured that his loading and unloading work gang will also join the duties. Bihari finishers known as 40 thieves also assured that they are not afraid now and cannot wait for arrival of Dr. Samant indefinitely.

I did not have a problem in running of paper machine. Mr. Rao, Mr. P. K.Chopra, J.K.Mathew and Akhilesh Sharma chief engineer R.K.Maheswari and electrical Engineer R.C.Maheshwari assured me that paper makers, shift in charges and engineers were capable of running the machine and they would work day and night. They were all members of staff.

I called the security contractor Tiwari and asked him to bring 250 workers for three months. I would pay them full three month wages even if my regular labour force joined next day. He brought 150 workers who were whisked in factory in the darkness of night. Since all the preparations were made as per my plan I decided to start the factory on 3rd January 1989. M.D., Mr. Rao, Mr. Chopra and Mr. Mishra knew this fact. We had not disclosed the date to anyone else even to my wife.

My father-in-law who had treated me earlier in 1968 had gone to Madras for his bypass surgery. He was staying in our Madras Office. My wife received a call from my brother—in-law that his surgery was to take place on 3rd January 1989 and he wanted me to remain present with him at that time. He was 77 years of age at that time. My wife started making the preparation to go to Madras as she was unaware of my plans. I had no other alternative except to disclose my plans. I explained to her that if I leave the colony at this time the whole plan will fail. Boiler operators will not join. Security contractor will not bring the workers. Members of staff will be demoralized. Though my father-in—law had treated me and in time of his need I should have been present besides him at the Hospital at Madras but I considered my first duty towards mill and its employees for whom it was the question of survival. She understood as I had always seen her as a very cooperative person whenever such a dilemma took place in past too. She also realised that she should not leave the colony I started the factory on 3rd January 1989. Outside striking workers said to their members that management was only burning bagasse so that smoke comes out of boiler chimney. They said this was being done to demoralize them. Next day paper machine was started. Finishers also joined the duties. Jha babu saw that they give maximum output. All the members of staff, irrespective of senior or junior, worked in 12 hours shift. I converted the office of M.D as my bedroom. I started visiting factory several times in odd hours of night to encourage them and create a sense of security.

Workers moved to industrial court and obtained a stay order on recruitment of fresh worker. They gave it to district authority and requested to close down the factory.

District Authority issued a show cause notice. My Lawyer explained the stay order was applicable from the date of the order. Worker recruited before that date are not covered and we gave an undertaking that from the date of stay order we will not recruit any worker.

This way we worked for one month. More skilled workers joined. Now I know that it was a matter of few days when all the workmen would join their duties.

K.K. Babu visited factory during this period. He wanted to see what was going on in the factory. On his rounds he smiled and said to all the senior managers that he had never seen so much cleanliness inside factory earlier. He was happy to see factory running in a most efficient way with casual workers.

However the leaders made a last attempt to keep the morale of striking workers high. They distributed the copies of the letter on the letterhead of union informing that Dr. Samant had finally decided to address a meeting on a particular date.

The date was 15 days away from the date of distribution of leaflets. Workers working inside showed sign of fear. There was uneasiness. Mr. Rao and Mr.Chopra informed me about this development. I had myself observed this phenomenon during my rounds. These fifteen days time was a trying time for all of us who were working inside. I had a meeting with Mr. Rao, Mr.Chopra and all the senior managers and engineers. All the important people started staying in factory on duty during night time. Security contractor Mr. Tiwari, Dayaram Seth, Isamil Wahab also made it a point to be present in night. K.K. Babu also took night rounds during his visit. This created confidence amongst the workers. At the end of appointed date

Dr. Samant did not appear. There was a fight amongst leaders and workers who were up till now believing their leaders. I knew then that strike had come to an end.

Now workers wanted to join. They were leaderless and did not know how to approach the management. I did not want to miss this chance. With the help of Dayaram and Mohan son of our very respected boiler operator Sardarji I sent a message to them that management believes in the policy of forgive and forget and they were welcome provided they join their duties within three days otherwise their services will be terminated. All joined their duties the next day. Mohan led the group. This way the strike ended on 25th February 1989. I made full payment as per my promise to all the workmen who had come from outside. I thanked God for helping me again. All the managers and industrialist of Jalgaon heaved a sigh of relief. K.K. Babu felicitated me. He also issued a letter of appreciation of my services

INAUGURATION OF A "PYAUU"

Shri Laxminaryan Bajaj father of my co-brother was having an unexplainable affection for me. He was a kind-hearted man. He constructed a pyauu (a place where cold drinking water is available) in cloth market of Ujjain. He wanted I should do the inauguration. I visited Ujjain in 1988 and inaugurated the pyauu.

Shri N.L. Mishra, Commercial Manager

It will be unjust on my part if I do not write few lines about this elderly gentleman. He had joined us in August 1982 when his age was 59 years. He had worked earlier in GRASIM, Nagda. He was very disciplined person. He was elder in age to me but had never questioned my instructions to him. He played a very important role during strike period. I had given him the responsibility to see that all the outside workers get three meals in time so that they were not late on duty. It was a difficult job. First we decided to give Puries in all the three meals but many workers fell sick. Later he made arrangement of Chapaties. Within 2-3 days he regularized every activity of temporary kitchen. He attended duty early in the morning at 6 am. and never left before 10 pm till all the workers had taken their meals. He had thus relieved me of a very important work.

All the ladies accepted Mrs. Mishra who was an elderly lady in the colony as universal mother-in—law. She was very helpful to newly wed couples. But she was very strict in observing Indian culture. No lady dared to come to her without covering her head. Unfortunately Mrs. Mishra died at the age of 83. Mishraji is still alive and has completed 87 years of age. He is staying alone in his flat in Jaipur.

SMOOTH WORKING THEREAFTER

After the strike workers realized their mistake. Mill started working smoothly. We had repaid almost all the loans. Only working capital bank limits remained. K.K. Babu started concentrating on erection of recovery boiler. In the middle of the year I heard that talks of division of property are taking place between both the brothers.

Shri N.K.Somani who was the elder brother and chairman and K.K. Babu who was younger, started negotiation. These were the months of uncertainty. However I knew this fact only.

The Mill was running very efficiently. We had earlier received many prizes one after another.

In 1985 we received the first prize as National productivity award.

In 1985 again we received first prize for making best use of production capacity. Award was given by Association of National Paper production.

In 1986 again we received the above award.

In 1986 we received award for energy saving.

In 1987 we received second prize for making best use of production capacity.

In 1987 again we received prize for energy saving.

In 1987 IBPL gold medal for energy saving.

1988-89 IBPL first prize for energy saving.

1988-89 Certificate for best use of production capacity.

Partition and my departure from Bhusawal

By August 1990 it was clear that division has taken place. K.K. Babu was given the owner ship of Nasik factory. Now it was known as Soma paper and Industries.

Shri N.K. Somani took possession of Shri Vindya Paper Mills Ltd Bhusawal. I knew N.K.Somani very well. He called me and asked me to stay with him. He was an Ex. M.P and had very good contacts. He was a well read person. He had written few books and also translated in Hindi the famous book "Vendanta Treatise" of Shri A.Parthasarthy.

I also understand that his son Shekhar Somani will manage daily work. He was younger to me, and a very well behaved person. I was sure that I would not have any problem from their side.

I had worked with K.K. Babu for a long time. I liked his decision making process. He never kept any files in his cabin. I thought that I would not be comfortable to work with Shekhar Somani who never took fast decisions. I had seen his table full of papers. He had any space on his desk left to write or sign. But I admire his sense of memory. He could find out any document within seconds from the heap of papers on his table. Though I was the most senior most employee, with good salary and other facilities I resigned in October 1990 at the age of 51 years and told them that I wanted to start my own business. Shri N.K. Somani accepted my resignation. Mr. V.Sheshadri Rao was appointed as General Manager and Mr. P.K.Chopra as the Deputy general Manager. On 31st December 1990 I was relieved of my responsibilities as the General Manager of Shri Vindhya paper mills for which I had given precious ten years of my life, living alone for 5 years and fighting a battle in the remote village risking my life. I shed tears while packing my luggage. I thought how much more painful the decision of division must have been for K.K. Babu who had made this mill a success out of nothing. From this day the down fall of their family started. I left Bhusawal on 31st Dec. 1990 for Nasik with my bag and baggage.

This is the end of my story from 1981 to 1990.

PART FOUR

My life story
from 1991 to 2012

I came to Nasik with my wife in January 1991. Sundeep was in USA and Amit was in Pune in third year of Computer Engineering course. I rented a office at Upnagar, Nasik. I also took on rent a godown near my office.

My flat was on the third floor in a society. I felt something was amiss. In the mills I was staying in a small bungalow but that was having huge open space for garden where I would grow vegetables etc. Here I had to stay on the third floor. However K.K. Babu appointed me as a Director in Soma Paper Nasik.

Both the Somanis viz N.K and K.K were kind enough to grant me the distributorship of paper of Bhusawal and Nasik factory. There was intense competition. I was getting only Rs 500 per ton as commission. One truck of 10 M.T. of paper was costing about 3 lacs of Rupees and commission was only 5000. It was only 1.6%. Somehow I managed to sell about 100 ton a month. I was earning 50,000 per month which was just enough to meet the expenses.

I had three very loyal employees with me. Mr. Bhalerao had worked at Vindhya paper Bhusawal. He left the services and joined me. I explained to him that it was not a wise decision on his part. He was working in a Limited concern and to join a partnership business was not wise. He insisted to join me and resigned from Vindhya. I had no other alternative except to take him with me. I could manage to pay the salary he was getting in Vindhya Paper.

Second one was Kamal Kishore Jhawar who was the son of Stores officer Shri Jhawar who had worked with me during my service with Vindya Paper Mills Nasik. He was at that time completing his ICWA course. He passed intermediate examination. I explained to him that he should complete the course and join some good company but he insisted in joining me.

Third was my nephew Shikhar who had passed B.Com and came to stay with me. My friend Mr. Sunder who had by this time retired from HAL supervised all these three people's work.

I started the business. I was covering expenses but not making any substantial profit. I wanted to pay a good salary to all these three boys even if I do not get any amount for me. That way I was doing well.

Once in 1992 in connection of business I visited Silvasa. I learned that being a backward union territory there was no tax on paper. I purchased a godown there approximately of 2100 sq. ft. I also brought this fact to the notice of management of Shri Vindhya paper mills. They agreed for stock transfer and I could sell material in Silvasa. That way my sales improved.

In 1993 Amit completed his engineering course. He also started assisting me. He was very systematic. But still I was not satisfied. My intension to start business was to just pass time but now since I have to make the future of above three persons I once again started working seriously. Silvasa business was showing good results I therefore transferred my nephew Shikhar to Silvassa with independent charge. He showed good results. But still two type of customers used to come to me. One those who wanted the material urgently. It was not a problem for me as Mr. Chopra who was now the general manager was quite accommodative. Second those who thought that they would get special quality of material because of my past. It was not possible so they purchased only once but after realizing the fact they did not approach me. I too did not encourage these types of customers. Now Bhalerao, Kamal and Amit were with me. They were looking after the business. I was not having much work to do.

REGISTRATION OF TRUST

Once in 1982 when I visited Mumbai Office. In order to satisfy my curiosity I had asked K.K. Babu about his family trust. The name of the Trust was 'Hazarimal Somani Memorial Trust'. They were running schools, colleges and hospitals in this Trust. I specifically asked about the source of income. He explained that they are contributing certain percentage of profit from their all the businesses to this Trust. I thought I must do some work for society may be on a very small basis. I requested Shri O. K.Somani C.A to submitt application for registration. He drafted the trust deed. My elder brother Narendra Kumar Gupta became the settler. The name of the Trust was given on my father and grandfather's name. In place of Gupta we decided to register it in the name of our Gotra, which is Goyal. Thus the name of the trust was Badriprasad Nemichand Goyal Charitable Trust. Since I was not in any hurry we did not follow the matter till charity commissioner himself called us. Eventually the trust was registered. Later when it was registered I considered this as a futile exercise. What a charitable work could be done with meager amounts I was contributing to trust. I was not in the habit of asking donations from outsiders. At that time I did not realize that it was the wish of God who wanted me to have a registered Trust for the future work that was to be carried out by me in his design of plans for me.

MARRIAGE OF SUNDEEP

In October 1992 my elder son Sundeep wrote me a letter that he wanted to marry a girl who came in contact with him in San Francisco. The girl was also a software engineer. She was a Bengali Girl. Her name was Anasua Munshi. She had graduated with a B.E in Electrical from Government College Pune and M.S in Image Processing and Micro processing from University of Missouri Columbia in USA. Her father was the Deputy General Manager of TELCO Pune. Her mother was in USA in those days. I called her and agreed for the marriage.

She came to India in January 1993. We discussed the plans of marriage, which was fixed on 5th January 1994. This was the first marriage in the second generation of my family. All the relatives and friends attended the marriage. All Somanis from Bombay came to attend the marriage. Shri J.T.Mahajan the then home minister also attended the marriage.

Sundeep has been blessed with a son named Karshin on May 20th, 2000, a daughter Karinna on January 4th 2002 and second daughter Kaylika on 12th January 2006.

My first visit to USA

The first time I visited USA with my wife in the year 1995. It was a short visit of 42 days. I started on 5th July 1995 and returned on 11th August 1995. I had read a lot about America. I had read western novel of Louis L'Amour and many other writers. I wanted to see Niagara Fall, Disneyland, Grand Canyon, Hollywood, Texas, Las Vegas and other places. When earlier I visited Europe I had written my liking for travel by train so that inland of a country can be seen. I asked Sundeep to purchase Amtrak (National Rail Road Corporation) travel card and reserve a sleeper cabin for my wife and me for 21 days. My daughter in law Anu made my tour program and Sundeep arranged all the reservations in train and hotels. I started my journey by train from San Francisco to Seattle.

We stayed here in a hotel for one day and visited city and other places of interest. It is a very cold place. From Seattle we travelled to Chicago. We crossed Idaho, Montana, Dakota, Minneapolis and Wisconsin and reached Chicago at 8 pm over three hours late. By this time we missed our connection to Washington. Amtrak people started contacting us almost two hours before the train reached Chicago. They offered me two seats on other train starting at 11pm but without sleeping arrangement. I informed them I could not travel sitting whole night and the train would reach the next day evening. I would not make my reservations for site seeing. They realized my difficulties and made my night stay arrangement in a hotel and gave me an air ticket by morning 8 am flight to Washington. They also arranged a taxi from hotel to Airport. I reached Washington before my train in which I had to travel originally from Chicago. Thus I could maintain my sightseeing program. Countryside America is beautiful. We crossed big rivers like Mississippi and Missouri, great falls, forests, mountains and desert. The breakfast, lunch and dinner was provided in the train itself that was included in ticket.

From Washington we travelled to Raleigh in the state of North Carolina to stay with my sister's son Sunil Jain. He and his wife Renu gave us a grand welcome. Renu prepared various Indian dishes, as she knew that I was fond of eating. She also thought that since we had been travelling for a long time we might have missed Indian cuisines. They prepared many sweets like Jilebi and Gulabjamun and snacks like Samosas, Bhajias, Puris and Kachoris at their residence. They took us on a tour of the city. We enjoyed our stay with theme. This place was very hot. We stayed only for one day and came back to Boston and from Boston to Buffalo. We stayed in a hotel and travelled to Niagara Falls by a taxi about 23 km. We took a ride in a boat called "Maid of the Mist" that took us right below the falls. We also saw the great whirlpool six kilometers down side of falls. From Buffalo we again came back to Chicago. My Brother-in-law Dr. Deepak Agrawal (My wife's cousin) received us at the Chicago station and drove us in his car to West Lafayette, Indiana. He used to teach in Purdue University at that time. He showed us the University campus. I had earlier seen the campus of Banaras Hindu

University. However this University had a very big campus. All the Universities of America have good facilities and a vast piece of land at their disposal. Here one boy greeted Deepak as "Hi Deepak". When I inquired about the boy, Deepak informed me that he was his student. In India we address our teacher as 'Sir'. Deepak read on my face some kind of surprise, therefore, he clarified that in America people are informal. They do not believe in formality. Here a son-in-law calls her mother-in-law by her name. Like "Hi Jenny! how are you?"

The Next day he again drove us in his car to Chicago. We enjoyed our stay with him. I got to see a bit of Midwest of US or the heartland. Geographically, it can be compared to MP of India.

From Chicago we came to Grand Canyon in the state of Arizona. It is the largest canyon in the world. At the bottom of the canyon is Colorado River. It is the roughest river of America. It was an interesting journey by train. We crossed Missouri, Great Plains of Texas. We saw herds of buffalo and cowboys. We crossed Santa Fe Trail on which mules driven trains were running for travelling east to west before railroad was introduced.

From Grand Canyon we travelled to Disney Land. In Disney Land we enjoyed almost all the amusements. From here we travelled to Las Vegas by train crossing part of Nevada desert. I imagined how people had crossed it on horses. We stayed in hotel MGM Grand, which has 5,000 rooms. This was my first experience of staying in such a big hotel. I travelled in a bus through Las Vegas city and saw famous casinos the names of which I had read in books. I was surprised to see such a vibrant city in the center of a desert. We stayed two days in this hotel and enjoyed casino.

From Las Vegas we had to start in the morning by 9 am train. But due to some reasons the train was cancelled. Railway authorities arranged two A.C buses for Los Angeles. We reached there at 6 pm again travelling through the desert. It was an enchanting journey. In Las Angeles we visited Universal Studios. We took a drive through studio in a bus they call it a tram drive. We were shown how 'Jaws' was filmed. It was filmed in a pond of 100ft by 100ft. How Moses crossed sea in Ten Commandments. They have still preserved King Kong. How the bicycle ride in film 'Extraterrestrial' was filmed. They showed many tricks which look real in film. We also took a tour of Hollywood.

From here we travelled to San Diego to visit Water world. Perhaps the key underwater view is a tunnel that takes visitors underneath the shark tank. We also saw the famous 'Bay watch' live show on San Diego beach.

Lastly we returned back by train to San José, a railway station south of San Francisco where from we had started our journey. Countryside America is entirely different from its cities. It has still preserved its western image. Inside the villages there are still wooden electrical poles on which cables hang. There are cabins in forest and mountains. Horses are being used in remote areas. We saw many Indian settlements. In short we enjoyed our journey by train. Later I also visited USA in 1998 and 2002 and 2008 and visited many places including reserve forests and parks.

REAL BREAK IN BUSINESS

One day in 1995 when I was sitting in my office one of my old acquaintance Mr. Raman came to see me. He was working as a chief control officer in India Security press Nasik. I knew him since 1978 when I was the chairman of Rashtriya Navratri Utsav he was in one of my committees. He informed me that they were in need of post card paper. The supplier who was supplying the material was unable to fulfill his commitment due to strike in his factory. There was a hue and cry about the short supply of post cards. They were every day reminders from Post and Telegraph Department.

I sent with Mr. Bhalerao the sample of post card paper to Mills. Mr. Chopra informed me that the paper could be made. I telephoned to Mr. Raman next day morning that I can supply the paper. In the afternoon of the same day he arranged my meeting with the then General Manager of India security press Mr. Pant. He was quite honest while discussing the matter. He asked me to submit quotation. I submitted the quotation the next day. I did not ask, though knowing well about their urgency, more rate than what the present supplier was supplying. He issued a supply order for 300 tons of post card paper with the condition that only 10 tons would be supplied first and on approval balance quantity would be supplied. However on rejection of this 10 ton I will have to lift the entire material at my cost and the order would stand cancelled. I agreed. We supplied first lot of 10 MT. The works manager was my friend, who was the chairman of Souvenir committed during the festival of Rashtriya Navaratri Utstav that had taken place in 1978. He took extensive trials and gave the approval report to G.M. who in turn gave me green signal to supply the balance material. I completed the supply in 12 days. There was so much scarcity of post card that they had to run machine 24 hours for printing. The G.M Issued additional order of 300 MT and that too was completed within next 15 days. India security press authorities were happy. This was a real break for me.

Again I was called to supply Inland Letter paper. It is ordinary paper in blue colour. There was no problem for the mill to manufacture this paper. I during the period of six month got 1200 tons order from India Security press and Government printing press Hyderabad.

Thereafter I supplied many types of papers regularly to them during 1996 to 1999.

PURCHASE OF PLOTS OF LAND AND CONSTRUCTION OF BUNGALOW

During 1995 I purchased a plot for construction of my bungalow. Originally there were three plots. Two approach roads were dividing these three plots. Total area of these three plots was 2500 sq yards. Area of road was 240 sq yards. I purchased all the three plots and asked the developers to submit a new layout without roads. He removed the roads and joined all the three plots. He gave me 240 yards as free of cost. Thus I got 2740 sq yards against my payment for 2500 sq yards. I constructed a bungalow on one plot of 900 sq yards and kept 1840 sq yards on the backside of bungalow as open space for garden and kitchen garden. I planted eight coconut trees, one chickoo tree, one star fruit, two mango trees, one bel fruit tree, two lemon trees and some seasonal fruit trees. I kept some area for vegetable garden in which I am growing all type of vegetables.

In 1995 I also purchased two plots with a combined area of 1100 sq yards. These plots are in a strategic location connecting Nasik with Nasik Road.

In May 1997 I shifted my residence and began living in the newly constructed bungalow. Life was beautiful again. My new house was just 2 km from my office. I was also able to enjoy my hobby of cultivating vegetables.

In 2001 I undertook construction of my office cum godown and two flats on first floor. The building was completed in February 2003

SUDDEN SHOCK FROM AMIT

Suddenly Amit decided to proceed to USA for further studies. He was not happy with this trading business. I think I had committed some mistakes. First I had not given him free hand. Secondly I did not cooperate with him for starting a small scale Industry. He was disturbed for some time. I finally decided to allow him to do whatever he wanted to do. In January 1999 he left India for further studies.

His departure to USA disturbed all my plans. Now I feel God wanted me to undertake ultimate work he had fixed for me.

My wife started showing the signs of depression. My office building was complete. I constructed one godown at ground floor 25x25 sq. ft. My office was on mezzanine floor, two large rooms of 25x12 ft. each on the first floor and one hall of 25x25 ft. on the second floor. My plan was that many teachers were taking tuition classes at their residence. They are giving lessons to 10 to 15 students in a congested room in their residence. I decided to give them the rooms and hall for teaching on shared basis. I fixed 30% of the fee they were charging. I thought they would be able to teach 20 to 30 children in the same time in bigger rooms with proper arrangements for sitting and a Black Board. However no one liked this idea. It was more convenient for them to teach at residence, while performing their other routine work. My plan failed.

Since Amit had left I also lost interest in paper trading. As I had earlier predicted that down fall of paper mill would start, it started in 1999. I stopped submitting tenders because I was not sure of supply of paper. I therefore decided to wind up the business. I gave the ownership of my Silvasa business to my nephew Shikhar. The ownership of Nasik business was taken over by Kamal under a new entity. I closed my firm totally.

In 2003 Mrs. Supriya Kamath retired from St. Xavier High School. She started summer camp in one of my office Hall. She had a long tenure in St. Xavier School. She was quite popular amongst students and parents. She was dedicated to the cause of education. During her camp of 15 days I had frequent interaction with her and found her a dynamic lady. She also met my wife. She suggested that I should open a school. I hesitated, as I was not conversant with running of a school. I was a teacher but that was 40 years earlier. She assured me that she can run a primary school up to 7th standard in this building. She also suggested me that my wife would also show improvement in company of small children.

She arranged all the application forms. School permission required charitable trusts. Fortunately I had already registered a charitable trust.

She filed the necessary application form. My application was forwarded to Director of Education Pune who recommended and forwarded it to Government of Maharashtra at Mumbai. We were waiting for the permission to come. I was not serious about running a school therefore I had adopted a casual approach. Many of my friends whom I told about starting a school and my application advised me to follow up the matter with education department at Mumbai. They further warned me that getting permission is not an easy job. I did not pay any heed to their advice. I have written earlier that God wanted to give me the ultimate work he had fixed for me. I received the permission in 2004. My friends were surprised. We started the school.

FIRST BUILDING OF GOLDEN HORIZON SCHOOL

First building of Golden Horizon School

220

Starting from Nursery, Jr. KG, Sr. KG and 1st standard. We got fairly good number of students. Mrs. Kamath appointed good English speaking attractive young girls as teachers. She told me that a child always tries to find her mother in their teacher; therefore a teacher should be of the same age of mother. My wife also started attending the school full time from 8.30 am to 2.30 pm. She would sit in the Nursery with children up to 12.30 and then with Mrs. Kamath in her office. In nursery when children come for the first time to school they feel insecure as they are parting with their mother.

They start crying and take almost one month to settle. During this period children were happy to find a lady of the age of their grandmother. They used to come to her and sit around her. Some time my wife would tell me that she had not wiped the nose of her sons so much as of these nursery children. She started enjoying her time with little children. She showed sign of improvement.

So the very first year both the halls at first floor and one hall of godown was fully occupied. Soon after submitting application I had divided godown in two halls and above it a mezzanine floor reducing the height of godown. On this mezzanine floor she kept games purchased from Mumbai for Nursery children.

Next year 2005 we started second standard. It was started in the Hall at second floor. Now I was having a fairly good idea about school. I realized that in this building running school up to 10th standard would not be possible.

I asked Mrs. Kamath how would it be possible to accommodate all the classes in this building. She suggested placing a partition in the hall that could accommodate up to 5th standard. For 6th to 10th standard we would run a second shift.

Mrs. Kamath was a very inflexible lady. Whenever I gave any suggestion her first reaction would be a refusal. I therefore, so many times, while giving any suggestion to her started adding 'no' as her answer for the sake of fun. She would laugh. I too was very assertive during my whole career and in spite of controlling myself I had hot discussions several times with her. She was very friendly with my wife and I am thankful to her for treating my wife well. However in the month of November 2005 she gave me a shock when she informed me her decision to resign. Perhaps she thought it was not possible for her to work with me. She told me that she had to go to Australia as her daughter-in-law is expecting her first child. I showed my willingness to grant her leave for 3 to 4 months. But she was not sure if she would return so early or even within one year. She told me that she had plans to settle there with her son.

She assured me that she will put someone equally experienced and dedicated lady in chair. She called two to three ladies for interview. She finally called Shaila Thomas who had worked for nearly 18 years in St. Xavier Jesuit School. We selected her to take the reins from Mrs. Kamath.

Mrs. Kamath left us from 31st March 2006, I still respect her as the promoter principal of "Golden Horizon School".

My intention in starting the school was to give quality education to children of lower middle class families. My fee structure was the lowest. Dividing the hall would result in no space for extracurricular activities. I also came to know that quality schools are running in one shift.

SECOND BUILDING OF GOLDEN HORIZON SCHOOL

Second building of Golden Horizon School

I decided to construct a second building on my second plot in October 2005. My architect Mrs. Archana Pekhale who had made the drawing and design of the first building completed the drawing of this second building. We started construction subject to approval of plans by Corporation. It was as per the requirement of school. It had 12 rooms, one hall at 1st floor, staff common room, kitchen and two store rooms. Spacious urinals and toilets were provided on each floor separately for girls and boys. I wanted from 1st to 10th standard classes in this building, remaining each room would accommodate Computer and Science Laboratory. She submitted the plans to Nasik Municipal Corporation in November 2005 and started construction simultaneously. NMC approved plans on 14th February 2006. The construction was to be completed within one year. I too wanted to complete it before next academic season. She gave me an estimate of 40 lacs. In Murphy's law I had read that estimate given by Architect should be raised straight way by 50%. So I wanted Rs. 60 lacs. It was a serious problem for me. I had spent the total amount earned from business in constructing my house, purchase of these two plots for school buildings and in construction of building number one.

I calculated all my savings in shares, deposits and mutual funds. The main investment of 30 lacs was in shares of different companies and 12 lacs in deposit and mutual fund. Now I was in real difficulty. If I sell all these investment even then I would be able to collect only 45 lacs. How the balance of 15 lacs will be arranged, was a difficult question to answer. I had never taken bank loans and was not inclined to take a loan and disturb my sleep. Another question I asked suppose I managed a loan of Rs 20 lacs from my son Sundeep and completed the building how will I pull on my house expenses. The school was not in position to generate surplus to pay the rent for buildings. More over it was in a trust. I was not allowed to draw a salary. I realized that I was in hot waters.

I had no other alternative except to start the work. I started the work having full faith in God who will find out a solution to this problem. I always believed that this was the project of God who has fixed ultimate object of life for me. And He solved the problem. Suddenly in that year stock market started rising by leaps and bounds. The share of Larsen, which was purchased by me at 225 per share, rose to 3900 per share. I sold my total holding of 1000 shares. Similarly Grasim, which I had purchased earlier at Rs 400 per share, rose to 3800 per share. I sold 500 shares and few shares of Gillette, GSK Phrama, Colgate and Hidustan lever were also sold. This way I collected 60 lacs tax-free as Long-term profit was not taxable. I completed the construction in 8 months. The 2nd building was completed in June 2006 for shifting the primary school. I shifted the primary school in June 2006 in this building. Children were happy to sit in new classrooms. Now nursery section was having vacant space for children to play in the hall. Even after selling all the above shares market price of my investments remained over 30 lacs which was the original price at the time of start of construction. It was a miracle for me. Without touching my investment of 42 lacs I constructed a building of 10000 sq feet carpet area. The cost of construction came to 58 lacs

As soon as the new building was constructed, parents started believing in my promises. They knew if the child is admitted in Nursery they will not have to worry up to 10th standard. None of the teachers who had joined the school in 2004 left the services. That is most important from the point of view of parents. If the turnover of teacher is minimum, parents consider the school as stable. After construction of second building I did not face any problem of getting students. In fact now the pressure on admission has increased. Recommendation from politicians over phone and through letters started pouring in. Sometimes principal has to put extra chairs and tables.

MRS. SHAILA THOMAS

We selected Mrs. Shaila Thomas to take charge of the position of Principal of the school. She joined us on 1st May 2006. She is quite an experienced lady. Her qualification is M.A.,M.Ed. When she joined the school she had teaching experience of 22 years. She is quite committed to her job. In the beginning she was a little hesitant to take decisions, as she had not worked as a principal. She took no time in taking up the responsibilities and discharging them efficiently. I wanted a dedicated and qualified principal. Lack of experience and confidence was no criteria for me to worry. I had all the years in Vindya paper trained fresh engineers and commercial people. I supported and encouraged her. Outside administrative work was looked after by me directly through Mr. Bhalerao. Thus she could concentrate on academic side. In a few years she became very popular amongst the people of education department. They appointed her as a member of their inspection team. She started visiting various schools with this team and gathered knowledge. This way she has become a inseparable part of school. Later when she told me about her past, I realized that she had been quite dedicated to work. Whether it was winter or rain she gets up at 4 am. She will cook for her son and daughter and reach school at 8 am sharp. She used to leave school no earlier than 3 pm. Every day she travelled 25 km to attend school in city bus changing it three times during1985 to 89. Now she has purchased a car but her habit of getting up early in the morning is the same. She stays in Devlali camp and travels daily in her car about 15 km. Her husband Mr. Thomas is also working in our school office. Both are giving their best to school and very loyal to their cause.

PERMISSION FOR HIGHER SECONDARY SCHOOL

After the receipt of permission in 2004 for 1st standard, we received permission for next class every year. It is called natural growth of school. Thus in 2009 we added 6th standard. In this year an advertisement appeared inviting application for permission to start high school. I wanted to apply next year in 2010 when my 7th class will start. In receiving permission at least one year will pass and by the time I get permission in 2011 my 7th class students will be available to me for admission in 8th class. I thought if I apply in 2009 and get the permission I will have to start 7th and 8th standard simultaneously. For 7th standard I will have sufficient students as the students of 6th class of my school will be promoted. But getting students for 8th class directly would be a problem. However education department people advised me to apply now. They said who knows next year advertisement appears or not. This advertisement had appeared after a gap of 3 years. I therefore applied and prayed that the permission is delayed, but the permission came during the year itself so I had to start 8th class too in 2010 with only 12 students. But the Principal of the school was happy. She later told me that teachers will be able to pay proper attention to smaller number of students. This will be our first batch appearing for 10th standard. Due to the proper attention of teachers we will be successful in achieving 100% result. This will be feather in the cap of school. Our first batch will appear for Matriculation examination March 2013. I hope teachers will get proper reward of their dedication.

We added one new teacher every year. Teachers who joined us once never left. They are happy and satisfied.

I had seen that in many schools teachers have to approach education department for various permissions in addition to their duties of teaching. I relieved them of this duty. I advised the principal to concentrate on studies of the children. Mr. Bhalerao was appointed as the Manager of the Trust. He took care of outside work. He did the liaison work. Teachers were happy.

DEDICATION OF TEACHERS

Because of the hard work of teachers and able guidance of the Principal the school started getting laurels one after another. Teachers are very dedicated to the cause of education. They take extra efforts for the all-round development of students. Students see the glimpse of their mother in them and thereby teachers command well-earned respect. Many parents who occasionally meet me always praise the teachers of my school. I would specifically wish to write about one such incidence Narrated to me by a grandfather. Four grandsons of Mr. Ishwarchandra Damodar Rathod are students of my school. Out of the four grandsons two are the students of class 9th. One day in the evening he watched them play cricket. One child was bowling and another was batting. Suddenly after bowling the child cried 'out' and snatched the bat from the hands of the boy who was batting. The other one objected and said that he was "not out". Both started arguing. Suddenly the boy who had snatched the bat asked the other one to swear that he was not out. The boy said, "I swear by teacher Protima that I am not out!". The other boy without any more argument handed over the bat back.

Mr. Rathod told me that he was watching this from a distance. He added that when he heard the boy swearing by his class teacher's name he could not believe it and was overwhelmed. He added that in his childhood he used to swear by Vidhya

(Goddess of knowledge) or by mother but this was altogether a different experience for him. This was possible because of teacher's dedication to the cause of development of students and treating them as their own sons.

Marriage of Amit

Amit was now well settled but he did not think about marriage. His mother was insisting that he should marry. He had attained the age of 37. Finally he selected a girl. Her name was Maneesha Bendkhale. She is a Maharshtrian Vani (Vaishya) from Ratngagiri area of Maharashtra. Her father had retired as General Manager of Reserve Bank of India. They were settled in Mumbai. She had passed M.B.B.S from Grant Medical College Mumbai. She did some research work in Neurology and now completing her M.D. in General Medicine in USA. I never believed in caste and region. I agreed without any delay. Her father, mother and brother came to meet me at Nasik. I found her father quite an open minded person. Brother was educated and working as Manager in Tata Consultancy Services, a well reputed company. Mother is a simple house wife. His marriage took place in August 2008. I am happy to have one Bengali and other Maharashtrian daughter in law.

GOOD NEIGHBOR
MR. T.P.BHAGWAT

When I came to Nasik from Duskeda I met Mr.T.P Bhagwat who was the General Manager of Soma Paper and Industries. I had occasionally visited this mill, often during the visit of K.K. Babu and sometimes in connection with my paper business. I often met Mr. Bhagwat. I found him simple and helpful person. I developed a liking for him. When I purchased a plot for my bunglow I advised him to purchase one plot for him. He agreed and purchased a plot. Both of us constructed the bunglow simultaneously. I occupied it in May 1997 and he also occupied in the same month. Since then we are neighbours. He has two daughters. The elder one is Pooja is married and the younger one Geeta is to be married in March 2012. Both are intelligent girls. Puja did M.B.A and Geeta is an Engineer and MBA in Finance working in CRISIL.

Both of us always maintained that one should have good relation with his neighbor. Everyone would like to see a smiling neighbor every morning.

He is younger to me. When in 2002 I had gone for Angioplasty in Pune, he accompanied me. He stayed with me in Pune for 3 days till I came out of hospital.

He always accompanies me even if I go to hospital for my regular check up. Recently my wife had gone to USA for two months. He made it a point to send breakfast and Lunch every day. We meet every day in the afternoon in my kitchen garden. He irrigates the plants and help me in growing various types of vegetable.

We undertake morning walks together. Many a times jokingly he says that he is richer than me as he is holding white ration card. Colour of my ration card is saffron, which is issued to middle income group people.

MANOHAR GARDENS RESIDENTS WELFARE ASSOCIATION

When I purchased the plot for my bungalow The Chief City Engineer of Nasik Municipal Corporation was staying in a building near to my flat on the third floor. He told me the locality where I had purchased the plot was not a good place for people like me. I told him the locality is never good or bad. It is the residents who make the locality good or bad.

The locality has 90 plots for bungalows out which on 8 or 10 plots houses were constructed in 1998. Ours is a colony adjacent to military area and in the direct line of Military airport. Therefore there is restriction of height and only bungalows can be constructed.

One day I received a circular issued by one of the residents Shri Kanhaiya Kalani popularly known as Kanu. At that time his age might have been 34 years but when I met he seemed to be more matured than his age. He invited all the residents to his house to discuss the plans for the improvement of colony.

At that time there were no streetlights and roads were rough without tar on them. All the residents attended. We decided to join hands to improve the fate of this colony. We decided to register a residents welfare association. The name of the Association was given Manohar Gardens Residents' Welfare

Association. Brigadier Arvind Manohar Warty was elected as the chairman and I as a Secretary. Col. Ramchandran became the active member.

This was my first experience to work with a military officer and that too of a rank of a Brigadier. I found him very systematic and devoted to the cause. He was down to earth person and would not hesitate to appear before the officer of the lowest cadre in Municipal Corporation. It was because of his efforts that the look of colony changed from a deserted one to a posh colony.

In first two years the look of the colony changed. It was very easy for Brig Warty to get appointments from Municipal Commissioner. Our Corporator Shri Trimbakrao Gaikwad also helped us. He made extra effort to see that streetlights once sanctioned are fixed promptly. Tar roads inside the colony were made. A high-pressure pipeline for water was laid. In order to avoid the fluctuation in electricity supply a transformer was installed in the colony itself. In the later years job was easy. It was only to maintain a well-developed colony.

Kanu Kalani was a guiding spirit behind all these works. He suggested that we should make the colony green. We planted over 500 trees in the colony. Our Corporator Mr. Gaikwad arranged tree protectors. Our Association was awarded 1st prize by Corporation for planting of trees by us. It was a very active committee. We were meeting every month and the minutes of business transacted were circulated promptly to all the members.

From Brigadier Warty Col. Subedar took the charge as chairman. He tightened the security. We had one watchman in the day from 8 to 5 pm and one in the night from 10 to 6 am. He appointed a janitor for sweeping the roads and keeping colony free from plastics and litters.

In the year 2009 I have been elected as the chairman. Municipal corporation has changed the old streetlights with more illuminating lights, increased the height of polls to cover maximum area. Road that was built ten years ago had now many bumps and pits has been resurfaced. Both the sides of road paving blocks have been fixed. Our existing corporator Pratap Mehrolia is very cooperative. He has built a very good team of workers who look after the complaints of residents of his wards.

I have further tightened the security. Now it is available for 24 hour with one watchman in day and two in night with cell phone with them. Residents have willingly increased their monthly contribution for maintenance.

Temple of Laxminarayan

A temple of Laxminarayan was constructed. Shri Kanu Kalani mainly funded it. Kanu Kalani and I had gone to Jaipur to bring the Idols. Many people of nearby colonies are visiting every day to have darshan.

In our colony now 11 colonels, 2 Brigadiers have constructed their Bungalows and one Major General owns a plot. Others are business people and executives. All the residents are quite disciplined because of Military people.

Our colony has become a posh colony in Nasik Road. Everyone wants to purchase a plot here but nobody is ready to sell. Every year we get an addition of 4 to 5 bungalows. Thus we proved that locality is made good by its residents and not by its mere location.

Shri Kanhaiya Kalani known as Kanu Kalani

He has also constructed a house in our colony. He is the man who took initiative for the development of this colony. When I came to know him he was only 34 year old. His father died when he was a student of intermediate. His relatives gave him two loss making factories. He had to leave his education half way. He has two younger brothers. How he turned both the loss making factories into profit making and how he settled his both the brothers is a fascinating story. Today he has 11 factories in Maharashtra and the biggest producer of Alcohol and allied products. He is always ready to help association by all means at his disposal. I was greatly impressed by this man. His wife Ritika is also very helpful to the residents. If any of the resident has any difficulty I always advise them to approach Ritika who will not sit silently unless their problem is solved. Kanu has two children one son and a daughter. Both of the brothers are working with him and have the same attitude towards life.

OUR FAMILY FRIEND MR VIJAY BHUTANI AND MRS VEENA BHUTANI AND WHY WE LIKE THEM

I met Vijay the first time in 1975. Both of us came to Nasik in the year 1974-1975. He was working in Paper Machine Wires Ltd in Satpur. I was working in Citric India Ltd. I do not remember how I came in contact with this family. I might have met him in one of the meetings of Nasik Industries Association. He is the person you meet once and become his friend. He is fond of parties. He had two school going children of the age of my sons. He was often inviting me with family to attend such parties. Mrs. Veena Bhutani is also a lady who mixes easily with other ladies. In her company my wife never felt lonely. In 1980 though I was transferred to Vindhya Paper Duskheda, he maintained friendship and visited Duskheda serval times to meet me. I also made it a point to enjoy his dinner parties whenever I came to Nasik. However in 1991 when I shifted to Nasik he was transferred to Chandigarh as the M.D of a paper mills. He came back to Nasik 1997 after leaving the job. We maintained the bond of friendship. On the face of events he looks an easygoing person. When I came in close contact with him I found him quite seasoned person. He settled his younger brother in Nasik. He arranged marriage of his younger sister though his own son and daughter had not completed their studies at that time. His father and mother stayed with him after retirement. His mother is still alive at the age of 85 and staying with him. Mrs. Veena Bhutani discharged all these responsibilities smilingly. I therefore became a great fan of this family. This was the reason why I blindly speak in his favour whenever occasion arises. People misunderstand me. One of them thought I blindly worship him. In his characteristic Hindi style he would say "Kyun Teli Tell Lagata Hai". He perhaps does not see the reason behind my devotion to this family.

He had arranged trips for his friends and families including my family. We had gone to Tirupati Balaji, twice to Malaysia, twice to Thailand, Kerala and other places. He has become our travel agent without any commission.

Through him I came in contact with many other families. I would like to mention few names. Vijay Shashtri, Narendra Kapoor, Suresh Jaisinghani, Anand Sitlani, Shankar kapoor, Prem Grover, Rajesh Ved and many others. I enjoy their company.

OUR PROJECT NAMED AS LAST BED (ANTIM SHHAYYA) 2009

Last bed

One evening when a few of my friends were enjoying a dinner party, I do not know how discussions took this turn and we discussed about the recent death of one of our common friend's wife. They had only one son who was out of India at that time. At least three days were required for him to arrive and join bereaved family. They decided to keep the body in public Morgue. This Morgue had its own limitation. They found the Morgue was stinking and plenty of rats were running around the place. They had to go through lot of time consuming formalities at the time of depositing the body and taking the body back. For a bereaved family it was very painful to go through such a situation and delays.

An idea suddenly came to my mind. Why we should not design a mobile morgue, which can be moved to the house of deceased. We made a casual survey and found that in our city alone, there were few thousand senior citizen who live alone and whose children and near relatives are overseas. They may need such facility some or the other time. Fortunately during my recent visit to a friend in Kerala, where almost all family members have relatives abroad, I found that they have come up with an ideal solution to this perennial problem. A group of social workers get together and arrange a mobile morgue, which can be sent to anyone in need.

Next day Narendra Kapoor and I visited several air conditioning shops but no one could provide us with the solution. Voltas peoples showed us their regular fixed morgue for keeping 5 bodies at a time. It was nowhere near our idea. One air conditioning shop owner agreed to make a box of our design which can preserve the body for 6 days below the minus 5 degree centigrade temperature. Size of the box was 6ft by 1.6ft x1.2ft. It was movable with 6 wheels. It worked. Later we reduced the length to 5.8ft and height 1.4ft width 1.2ft. We designed it in such a way that it could work with single phase electrical connection. Fitted with temperature meter, ELCB, volt meter and a tube light inside it and a transparent plastic lid.

The inauguration was done by Dr. Chahande who was the revenue commissioner of Nasik. Dr. Pankaj Gupta who was the president of Nasik Medical Association took special interest in this project and suggested that it should be given wide publicity. A leaflet giving its photo, technical details and how to operate it was printed and sent to all the doctors and hospitals of Nasik. Dr. Pankaj Gupta made extra efforts for its publicity. He visited with me the office of Times Of India and arranged a meeting of Journalists and reporters representing various newspapers of Nasik District. Times of India published a detailed article about this. Dr. Pankaj also helped me to prepare the leaflets. Instructions about how to operate it were prepared by Nissarbhai who designed and built the box. These are very simple. Only its plug is to be put in socket and switch to be put in on position. Within three minutes temperature starts going down and within half an hour it achieves—5 degree centigrade, which is sufficient to keep body for 5 to 6 days without any deterioration.

People liked the idea. I constructed a room behind my bungalow. Whenever people telephoned, my watchman used to give it to needy free of cost. Only they have to take it from my house and deliver it back after washing. I had also kept disinfectant to spray. Slowly people came to know about this facility. Telephone calls increased. Calls were always coming at odd time disturbing my sleep. It became increasingly difficult for me to manage the delivery late in night in winter and rainy season.

SHRI G.K.CHADDHA
A SOCIAL WORKER

Fortunately I met a person Shri G.K.Chaddha who had retired from Hindustan Aeronautics Ltd. His son is running a factory. Mr. Chaddha became a social worker. He is distributing lunch boxes free of cost in Civil Hospital and Ayurvedic Hospital every day. Both are Government Hospitals. Patients are getting food from Hospital but their relatives who are staying with them have to manage their food themselves. These are poor villagers who come for treatment from nearby villages. Mr. Chaddha is distributing free food packets. He saw this project. He organized people under the banner of Nasik Anna Seva Samity and rented a Gala. He kept this box there and giving free of cost thus catering the need of city. At Nasik road Shri Harish Bhai agreed to keep it in his Hotel compound where 24 hour watchman is on duty. He is so devoted that though he is an owner of a three star hotel sometimes he drives his delivery van in absence of a driver and gives the delivery of this box to needy.

Sindhi Association of Nasik and Devlali have made one similar box. One more box has been kept at Devlali donated by Shri Sharad Somani of Mumbai. All the people without any discrimination of caste and creed are using these boxes.

However I received feedback that all these boxes are useful for the people who are staying in a Bungalow or in a ground floor flat. Because of the length it is difficult to carry them to other floors like second or third floor as the landing space on staircase is not sufficient to turn the box. The box can be carried only in a horizontal position. Carrying it in vertical position will damage its compressor as oil may enter it. I discussed this problem with Nissar Bhai of swan refrigeration who made these boxes. He solved the problem.

He designed the box in three separate parts. One part is of compressor, second one is main body and third one is lid of acrylic sheet. Thus it was easy to carry and weight of individual part was not more than 10 kg. These are easy to assemble. Nissar bhai takes much interest in this project. He has become part of this project. He carries out repair work free of cost. One box costing Rs. 35,000 has been given by Shri Prem Grover from his charitable trust. Mr. Anand Sitlani contributed Rs. 10,000 for this project.

I am taught to reply 'welcome' whenever someone gives me thanks. In this case many users give thanks but I cannot say welcome.

My old friend Devichand and his daughter Ritu

In the April 2009 I visited Ujjain. I met Shri Devichand Sharma my old college mate. He took me to a Basketball complex being run by his daughter Ritu who is P.T. Teacher in a Government School. There are two courts of Basketball. I was impressed by the quality of courts and their maintenance. She wanted a water cooler for the children who come to play in summer season. I donated the water cooler costing Rs. 30,000.

A few months later when I again visited the place I saw some digging work going on. On my inquiry she informed that she wanted to construct a room for players to change their clothes. She had a plan to construct with asbestos sheets in absence of sufficient funds. I suggested her to construct two rooms with attached toilet and bath separately for girls and boys. I agreed to bear the cost. She sent an estimate of Rs. 3,20,000. I immediately sent the amount. In February 2010 it was inaugurated by the local M.P. I handed over the possession to the boys and girls.

Senior Madhvians' Meet

Recently in March 2011 a get-together of all the students of Madhav College who graduated before 1960 was organized in Ujjain. Shri Ramesh Dixit and Shri Satyendra Khandelwal made remarkable efforts in orgainising the meet and making it a great success. A Magazine "yaade aur yaade" and "karvaa yaadaon ka" (Memories and Caravan of Memories) was also published on this occasion. Many alumni attended. It was really an enchanting experience to meet former college friends after a gap of fifty years. We enjoyed meeting each other and remembering old college days. Good memories of those days were narrated. The total program was of eight hours with lunch break. Every one was delighted to meet their fellow students. Many lady participants in the meet who were hesitant to talk to us in their heydays of college were freely mixing with us. Nostalgia prevailed.

Now this get-together is being organized every year. Attendance is improving by leaps and bounds as every year condition of completing graduation is being relaxed by one year. While attending the program we travel through the time zone of our younger days and forget that time has travelled so fast that all this was fifty years ago.

SHARAD BAPAT
MY OLD COLLEGE FRIEND

I was having bigger plan for sports activity in Ujjain. I wanted to purchase land for conducting football and hockey tournament and coaching camps. I attended a gathering of old students of my college who had graduated in 1960 or earlier. Here I met my old friends. I invited them for dinner. Sharad Bapat, Shiv Singh Raguvansi and Devichand Sharma attended. I had with them discussion about the atmosphere of sports activities in Ujjain. I came to know that it lacks basic infrastructure for sports. Few grounds, which are reserved for sports activities, are regularly used for marriage, political activities or religious discourses. People call it pancho ka ground. Hardly any tournament is organized on these grounds. Sometimes people play just for exercise without any discipline. Old and young play together either cricket or other games wearing lungi or pyjamas. I gathered an impression that Sharad was the man who can fulfill my dream. Other two were always helpful in any activity. I left Ujjain the next day.

After a month I telephoned Sharad and told him about my desire. I found him very honest in giving advice to me. When I said I was ready to purchase land he informed me that inside city such a big piece of land was not available. If we purchase outside the city boys will not go that far to play. Days are gone when we were walking 10 to 12 km for playing games. Now children want a ground behind their house.

He sent me a more realistic and workable proposal. He proposed that he would conduct a coaching camp for 30 boys and girls below 19 year of age for 21 days. He will hire a school ground for this purpose.

1. In July he will conduct a football tournament for boys under 19 year of age and in November he will conduct Hockey tournament for boys and Girls in the age group of below 19 years.

2. From the tournament he will select 30 boys and girls and give them 21 days coaching.

3. He will provide the players necessary kit.

4. All the expenses of their refreshment, lunch, dinner and stay will be borne by us.

5. Winners and runners will be given cash prize. Individual players of winner and runner team will also be given cash prize. He gave me an estimate of Rs 1,20,000 /—for each year.

6. I agreed and sent him Rs 1,50,000/—keeping Rs 30,000/—for contingencies.

I agreed to send every year above noted amount for 10 years. I assured them that I am 72 year old and even if I am not there I will make arrangements from my Trust so that the amount is remitted every year. He conducted one coaching camp but unfortunately died of severe heart attack in December 2011. Thus I lost a good friend and a person committed to sports. I had insisted that he should keep the second line of organizers ready. I hope to hear from the young members of his team.

My two neighbours worth a mention here

Aruna and Maharajkumar Gupta an engineer are staying close to my bungalow. Renu and Arvind Gupta a commercial executive are staying adjacent to my bungalow. Our boundary wall is common. Both couples are much younger to me and treat me as their local guardian. They are great help to me and my wife. Aruna is one who sends Kachori in exchange for pumpkin. Renu readily mends my clothes. Our stock of pickles is never exhausted because of these two families. Whenever I need hot snacks, I have simply to ask them and they deliver it to me faster than Pizza outlet that too free of cost. It is a blessing to have such good neighbours.

MY WIFE SUMITRA GUPTA

My story is coming to an end. It is a success story of how a man through hard work and belief in God, has achieved more than he desired in his life.

Further here I would like to specially mention that behind "every successful man, there is a woman" but in my case besides my wife there are two men too, they are my sons. They too have sacrificed their need of a father with them, so that I could concentrate totally on my work. I hardly ever had any time to stay with them. The younger one Amit has always been closer to his mother, as she was the one with whom he had stayed, while I was away pursuing my goals.

I am proud to say that my wife Sumitra has inculcated all our traditional Indian values in them. My wife is a happy person who is a curious mixture of tradition with a modern outlook. She has happily embraced my daughters-in-law of different backgrounds as if they are her own daughters. She is a very affectionate lady who adores her grandchildren, Karshin, Karinna, Kaylie and the new entry is of Nia daughter of Amit and Maneesha.

She stood strongly by me in all the ups and downs of my life. She has supported me in achieving all my goals. My ultimate goal of being proud parent of two successful sons was achieved by her. The credit of bringing up two boys without my constant presence is laudable. My sons are my "Pride and Joy" and I am happy that they are happily settled in their respective households with their wife and children. I am again lucky that my sons have found highly qualified educated and affectionate soul mates.

My grandchildren are my future. I hope that they do well in their respective life. Karshin is a strappy lad, Karinna has grown taller than her mother and Kaylie is the baby of our house. The new entry is Nia who has made us ever happier. She was born in USA on 10th January 2012.

CHAIRMAN'S DAY

Happy birthday

Every year 7th of October, which is my birth day is celebrated as 'Chairman's day' by students, parents and teachers of my school. They assemble in school hall. They present an hour-long entertainment program. After entertainment program, each child shakes hand with me and then goes to his class where sweets are distributed to them. Every year they bestow me with so much love and affection that I feel blessed. I feel had my own children been here any two sets of parents and their four children would be celebrating my birthday. I feel lucky when I see 800 children, parents and teacher together celebrating my birthday.

THE BEST GIFT
I EVER RECEIVED

The best gift I ever received

I do not accept any gift and discourage parents sending flowers or bouquet. Once when my birthday was being celebrated one child of Jr. K.G. came to me after the program to shake hands. She gave me a chocolate. I found half a piece of chocolate when I opened it. Later I came to know that her parents had given the chocolate to her to eat during the program. She wanted to share it with me so in spite of being hungry she ate only half and saved half for me. What more can any one ask for? A child's love is a best gift from God given without guile or selfishness. It is fresh gift of innocence given to me through these innocent children. Again I feel blessed.

THE GRAND LODGE OF INDIA

I was the member of Rotary Club in the year 1978. A meeting of Rotary Club used to take place in Masonic Lodge of Devlali cantonment area. Here once a month some people calling themselves Masons, used to meet. They came to attend the meeting well dressed. Before the meeting began they would close the doors of the meeting hall tight and wear attractive regalia, collar and jewels. They addressed each other as 'brother'. They were business people, Doctors, Lawyers, highly placed Executives and other professionals. After the meeting they enjoyed dinner and drinks. They were very secretive and careful. Even on inquiry they would not disclose the purpose of their meeting. They would simply say "join the lodge and you would come to know." I thought they were propagating some kind of faith and meeting to enjoy refreshments. They called it "Banquet".

In the year 2008, one of my friends asked me to join the Lodge. Lodge no 358 was to be formed at Nasik Road. I was accepted for initiation. The Initiation ceremony is the ritual by which a member is admitted. During the ceremony of the first, second and final third degree, I came to know about the aims and objectives of Grand Lodge. It teaches about brotherhood of Man under the Fatherhood of God. It takes good people of virtue and makes them better. There the members are taught important duty they owe to God, to their country and the world as a whole. Thus the Grand Lodge of India makes its members as the responsible citizens of the world. They prepare their members as law abiding citizens of the world. The Lodge teaches its members first to become faithful and law-abiding towards their native country. I come to know that there is always an eternal struggle between good and evil, the temptation of life and triumph of good conscience. Life is full of evil including suffering, failure, sin, loss of friends and fortune, sorrow and death. These are our greatest problems and our severest tests. We must find wisdom to combat them and deal with win them over. Lodge teaches us how we should do this. We must raise ourselves above such evil and should not be a cause for such evil, thus making a happy world worth inhabiting. It teaches us that the evil in man must die, so that the good in man may live and triumph.

I was a new member though it was easy for me at this age to understand the philosophy but difficult to practice. However due to help, encouragement, brotherly love and affection and guidance of senior members it is becoming easy to practice. I have become an active member of the Lodge. Enjoying the meeting on every second Saturday of month and off course relishing the "Banquet."

LIFE NOW

I used to visit school and sit in my office every day from 9.30 am to 12.30 pm. Now I attend my office in school on 4 days in a week and that too from 9.30 to 11.30 am. My wife is also visiting school two days in a week just to keep in touch with students. She sits full time in Nursery for few days when it starts in June every year.

I pass my time in the backyard of my bungalow growing vegetables and distributing them in colony. Many a times I send fresh vegetable and get cooked one. There is a family to whom when I send Kaddu (pumpkin) the lady will invariably sends cooked vegetable with Kachori. In my garden I have kept two boxes for making manure by earthworms. I do not burn leaves or remains of vegetables instead I put them in these two boxes to be converted into manure.

I am not worried about my future. Both my sons have settled in USA, and they are happy there. I do not think much about them. My wife also is not thinking whether they will return or not.

In short I am enjoying the life. I am near nature as much as when I was a small boy and living in a closed ginning factory. I have created the same natural environment behind my bungalow. I have not developed any fancy garden. After many ups and downs life has become again beautiful.

I am enjoying my life with friends. Joining them for breakfast occasionally on Sundays. I have also joined a group of friends who meet once on every last Friday in a month on dinner.

I have joined investors club having membership of 50 persons who meet on every first Sunday of month. We discuss about stock market and other opportunities for investment in Nasik. I have known Madhu Maheshwari since 1977 when I visited Andhra Pradesh Paper Mills for the first time. Here again during the club meeting I came in contact with him and his wife Kamla Maheshwari. I also developed a liking for Satyaprakash Kela and his wife Susheela and Hari Maheshwari and his wife Sunita. All these families are staying alone like me. Their children are living abroad. We developed a liking for each other and started meeting once a month at each other's residence.

I have become a promoter convener of senior citizen club. We meet in Nasik club on first Friday of every month from 5 pm to 7 pm. In this club we organize picnic, lectures on heath and many other subjects and musical programs.

I have also joined a group of people undertaking morning walk every day on the artillery center road. We discuss each and every subject we can find. This group consist of Vasaantrao Nagarkar promoter chairman of Business Bank, Prof G.D.Nandre, Dr. Pagar, Ramesh Karle an ex-medical representative and now Yoga Guru, Vijay Mirajkar a developer,

Joginder Singh Saluja a hotel owner, Vinayak Godre known as K.T. No one knows for what name these initials stand. This club was named the Sunrise Club. A few more people joined us later. We meet once a month at the residence of one of the members to enjoy drinks and dinner.

I have gardening as a hobby. I have good friends. Teachers of our school love us. My wife treats them as her daughters. They are always ready to come to us in time of our need. Recently I had read an article written by Kushwant Singh about happiness. The article was circulated on the Internet. He explained what is happiness as:

1. You should have good health and understanding life partner.

2. You should not be depending financially on some one.

3. You should have good friends.

4. You should have a hobby to keep yourself busy.

5. You should own your house as a rented house cannot give you pleasure.

One more point I would like to add here. The happiest person is the one who can travel in memory lanes of his childhood during old age. Now I often dream playing in the closed ginning factory, playing on school and college ground, sitting in classroom with fellow boys and girl students and cycling in the outskirts of the city of Ujjain.

When my wife and I weigh us on the above parameters we find that we are happy people. Life has become beautiful again and golden period of my life has come back.

My story ends here but before I complete my story I am grateful to Somani family in general and Shri K.K Somani in particular who had a prominent hand in shaping my life. I dedicate my story to him with a sense of gratitude.

Shri K. K. Somani

THE END

Lightning Source UK Ltd.
Milton Keynes UK
UKOW03n0451201014

240307UK00003B/30/P